Creative
SERGING

Creative
SERGING

Innovative Applications to Get
the Most from Your Serger

Nancy Bednar &
Anne van der Kley

STERLING

New York / London
www.sterlingpublishing.com

PHOTOGRAPHY: K-Graphics, St. Charles, IL
ILLUSTRATIONS: Marthe Young
BOOK DESIGN: Richard Oriolo

Library of Congress Cataloging-in-Publication Data
Bednar, Nancy.
  Creative serging : innovative applications to get the most from your serger / Nancy Bednar & Anne van der Kley.
    p. cm.
  Includes index.
  ISBN 1-4027-1494-7
  1. Serging. I. Van der Kley, Anne. II. Title.

  TT713.B383 2005
  646.2'044--dc22

                              2004029964

10 9 8 7 6 5 4 3 2 1

Published by Sterling Publishing Co., Inc.
387 Park Avenue South, New York, NY 10016
© 2005 by Nancy Bednar & Anne van der Kley
Distributed in Canada by Sterling Publishing
c/o Canadian Manda Group, 165 Dufferin Street
Toronto, Ontario, Canada M6K 3H6
Distributed in the United Kingdom by GMC Distribution Services
Castle Place, 166 High Street, Lewes, East Sussex, England BN7 1XU
Distributed in Australia by Capricorn Link (Australia) Pty. Ltd.
P.O. Box 704, Windsor, NSW 2756, Australia

Printed in China

Sterling ISBN-13: 978-1-4027-1494-8 Hardcover
          ISBN-10: 1-4027-1494-7

          ISBN-13: 978-1-4027-4910-0 Paperback
          ISBN-10: 1-4027-4910-4

For information about custom editions, special sales, premium and corporate purchases, please contact Sterling Special Sales Department at 800-805-5489 or specialsales@sterlingpub.com.

Anne's Dedication

I would like to thank some of the remarkable women in my life who have nurtured, taught, and encouraged me to be where I am now. There is something special about the camaraderie of women that defies explanation.

To Mum for insisting that I finish my nursing education at a very low spot for me, so that I would have something to "fall back on," a possibility that was not really an option for her as the middle of 13 children in the years of the Second World War. It wasn't until I was a wife and mother with a new career in sewing that I was able to understand how lucky I was—and still am—that each day still sees me loving my work and looking forward to the challenges of the day and the future.

To Gai Haviland for being a tutor of the first order and stickler for doing it properly. To Janice Ferguson for being a mentor by accident and her unconditional help on my first teaching visits to the U.S., easing the way for me.

To those Queens and Goddesses who love sewing, serging, and embellishing with a passion that is shared and cannot be explained, to all the women who are developing their creative spirit just because they can, thank you. I am proud to be a member of the team.

And always, to the team at home, who support me no matter whether they want to or not, it just goes with the territory: Phil, Dirk, and Nina I won't promise that there won't be another book, I just am grateful that you have given me the opportunity three times already.

—ANNE VAN DER KLEY

Nancy's Dedication and Thanks

I'd like to dedicate this book to my wonderful children, Sarah and Adam. They both have been patient and understanding personal supporters in the midst of mountains of fabric, piles of paper and countless thread snippets that they and our dog regularly wear out the door. Supplying me with meals when I was too busy to cook, cleaning the house or offering creative input when I got jammed, they propped me up when I was too tired to go on. They never complained, always supported and for this I thank them. Love you, kids!

Thanks, also, to the editors of the now defunct Sewing and Serging Update Newsletter for giving me my first public writing assignments. They took a chance on an unknown writer and opened up a literary door I never thought was available to me. They challenged me with "what if" assignments and started me on a creative journey to break the rules and see what happens.

Thank you also to all my creative pals in the industry, Bernina staff and educators, fellow writers, suppliers who did not hesitate to supply me and Anne with countless supplies.

Lastly, I am grateful for my faith in a power greater than myself for getting me through these past few years. The road has not always been smooth, but somehow I got through. My talents, my inquiring mind and my wonderful children all stem from a place much larger than myself. I am humbled and thankful to be as blessed as I am.

—Nancy Bednar

Contents

Introduction

from Anne

WHERE DO I BEGIN TO explain the way this book came about? I had met Nancy on one of my teaching and book promotion trips to the US and immediately realized that she and I were both "sergerholics" of the first order. While the serger is not the only equipment in our sewing repertoire (yes, we can both do a ton of stuff at the sewing machine and computer, too), we both felt it was suffering from some tired ideas about what it was capable of in the twenty-first century with the next generation of sergers available with Coverstitch and Chainstitch. We corresponded through the magic of the Internet, and met whenever I was near Chicago.

I can't remember which of us started the "fabric challenge." We would buy equal amounts of the same outrageous or simply stunning fabric, me from Australia, Nancy on her travels stateside, and plan to challenge ourselves as to what we would do with it. Somehow, this idea took wing when we were celebrating our restraint (I had made only one credit card sob with distress at our personal fabric Mecca at Vogue Fabrics in Evanston, a suburb of Chicago). We were at a wonderful tapas restaurant we had discovered. Perhaps it was the second carafe of sangria that stimulated the creative *sergins* in us, but I know we sat there and drew up our book proposal on the spot.

As I write I am still astounded at how our book reflects so closely our sangria-enriched ideas: we have kept as true to the original ideas as we had planned, having to eliminate some projects because we just had far too many projects for this book. I hope our different styles, ideas, and projects stimulate you all to take a new look at your serger, and explore the textile art tool of the twenty-first century.

—ANNE VAN DER KLEY

from Nancy

Some relationships are just meant to be. I knew that Anne and I were kindred spirits from the moment I met her at a lecture she was giving here in the States. Striking up a conversation, we both realized that we were of a similar mindset regarding our thoughts on serging. There was much too much that had been repeated from the past and so much more available if we could just unlock the right creative door. We felt that we held the keys to open the way to urging serger owners to experiment and enjoy their sergers as never before. At a lunch break during a fabric-shopping trip, we were urged, with the help of a lot of excellent sangria, to put thoughts to paper. What if we wrote a book unlike anything else on the market? What would we put in it? How far could we push the creative limits? Hastily scribbling our notes on a napkin, I drafted a proposal and send it to my publisher, Sterling. They accepted it immediately and we were on our way. We thoroughly enjoyed our creative journey with the projects in this book and hope our readers do, too. It is our wish that they inspire you to dust off that serger box, reread your instruction manual and enjoy your serger.

—NANCY BEDNAR

Creative Serging

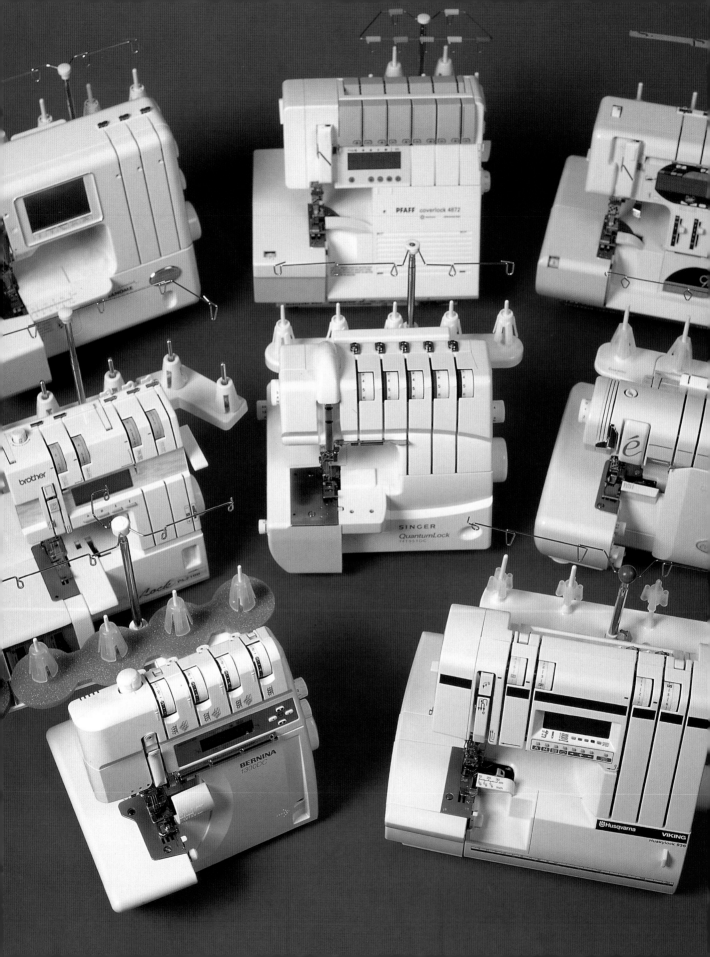

one

Parts of a Serger— Serger Models and Features

Parts of a Serger

You have your brand new serger fresh from the store and are chomping at the bit to get started. You have opted for the most creative serger available with coverstitch and chainstitch, the "next generation," combining traditional serger function with new versatile options. Read on and take a trip into the future with us. Why bother learning the parts of the serger and what they do? You have had a serger, or at least seen a serger before; surely this one cannot be that much different? You're thinking about taking the shortcut and just having a play, you'll read the instructions or learn the rest in your owners' classes later.

Sound familiar? I wish I could say I had not been down that particular road, but I was always advised by my mother to tell the truth!

How many ways can Nancy and I say that learning the parts and functions of your new serger is the easiest way of saving your precious time? By the time each and every control has been fiddled with, every door opened and every moveable part explored, time has flown out the door and you are generally no closer to starting to create. What started out as a shortcut has inevitably turned into a "long cut," with your saying once more that when all else fails, follow the instructions. Please remember, this is a lot of serger, one for you to grow into rather than grow out of. Spending a little more time now means a lot more play later

GENERAL OVERVIEW

Your new serger is really two sergers in one. There are variations with the different brands on the market but our criteria for selection was a regular serger setup also incorporating coverstitch and chainstitch within the machine rather than as a stand alone coverstitch machine. With that consideration in mind, the choices in the market fall into two general categories, either a 5-thread serger or 4-thread serger with coverstitch and chainstitch capability with all the regular serger functions we expect.

Read through the following guidelines while sitting at your serger and working with your manual (and perhaps some chocolate!). The next step on your creative journey is about to begin.

LOOPERS

The most obvious difference with the next generation of sergers with coverstitch and chainstitch becomes apparent as soon as you open the front cover: there is another looper, the chain looper. The extra looper adds to the versatility and function of this great equipment by offering stitches which previously were available only to industry. The chain looper sits in front and slightly to the left of the regular loopers, enabling stitches to be formed in the body of the work. The upper and lower loopers sit slightly to the right and behind the chain looper, with stitches forming along the cut edge of the fabric. The functions of the loopers is explained more fully below, with the stitches they create.

Regular Overlock

The upper and lower loopers and needles all interlock to form the stitch along the edge of the fabric. Threads are carried by the loopers which are "knitted" together over one or two pin-like protrusions called stitch fingers; the fabric keeps the threads separated, making each one readily identifiable. The upper looper threads form the top of the overedge or overlock stitch as they pass across the top of the fabric while the lower looper passes under the fabric forming the underside of the stitch. The needle threads hold, or "lock" the looper threads in position as the loopers are crossing each other. The knives are both engaged, trimming excess fabric in front of the loopers and needles to provide a clean edge over which the stitches form.

In all the sergers that met our criteria for inclusion in this book, you will have a 2-thread converter. This handy device sits in the eye of upper looper, temporarily disengaging it to provide versatile stitching with the minimum of thread for the finest stitching possible.

Combinations of needle positions, stitch finger widths, and selecting to use both loopers or just one looper create many stitch choices, both functional and decorative.

Coverstitch

Your coverstitch serger has a chain looper in addition to the upper and lower looper which travels in an elongated circular motion, from left to right, rather like an oval. The chain looper sits in front of the upper and lower loopers of the regular serger.

As it moves in the circular motion, the coverstitch needle(s) lower and interlock on the underside of your fabric as they form the stitch. The needle threads stitch on the top of your fabric and appear as parallel rows of stitching. The underside appears as a zigzag stitch with slight variations depending upon the number of needles or stitching width selected. Either side may be considered as the right side of the fabric depending upon the intended function or look desired.

Upper cutting knife.

The upper looper and knives are not used in this application; you will generally disengage both the upper cutting knife and upper looper which means that you can sew in the body of the project. In fact, Nancy and I both agree that this is the only time we ever disengage the upper knife.

The brands vary a little, with the choice of either 2-needle or 3-needle positions, giving you a choice of stitches. Wide placement of needles results in a wide coverstitch formation; a single needle results in formation of a chain stitch. If you have three needle positions available you have the option of the wide stitch, chain stitch plus a narrow stitch and one, two, or three rows of parallel stitching showing.

5-Thread Stitching

With both a chain and overlock stitch, this successful combination is most readily identified as the strong seam finish on the inside of jeans or ready-to-wear garments. The 5-thread stitch is worked with both the chain looper and chain needle forming the straight stitch; the upper and lower loopers and right or left needle form the overedge stitch simultaneously. The threading for the chain needle in this setup is a little different from that for coverstitch; the thread usually passes through a spring mechanism and gives a more taut stitch, best suited to construction.

This stitch is typically considered as the "industry" finish with a durable chain stitch seam and clean finish, meeting manufacturers' guidelines and consumer expectation.

Chainstitch

The chainstitch is created as either a stand-alone chain stitch at a 5-thread serger or by using one needle only from the coverstitch setup. In each instance, the needle penetrates the fabric and picks up the thread from the chain looper as it completes its circular motion.

The threading for the chainstitch at a 5-thread serger is a little different because of its role as an "industry" stitch; both the needle thread and the looper thread usually pass through a spring-type mechanism forming a stronger, more taut stitch, best suited to fabric construction.

No adjustments are needed to the threading path when using the chainstitch setup, with the resulting stitch being a little looser and the ideal for decorative serging.

NEEDLE POSITIONS

With two sets of loopers, your coverstitch serger also has two sets of needle positions. The regular serger function has a choice of two needle positions sitting at the right and slightly to the back of the coverstitch needles. Both needles can be used simultaneously or just one at a time, giving a choice of wide or narrow stitching. These needles interlock, or "knit" with the upper and lower looper.

The coverstitch needles sit to the left and front of the regular serger needles and give you a variety of stitch choices depending upon your particular serger. These needles interlock or "knit" with the chain looper. In general, those coverstitch sergers with two needles offer a wide coverstitch and chainstitch; those sergers with three needles offer a triple, wide and narrow coverstitch plus a chainstitch.

KNIVES

Your serger has two knives, one fixed lower knife and one moveable upper knife. The moveable upper knife moves against the fixed lower knife to cut. Think of a pair of scissors needing two blades to cut; this is the action your serger performs. The knives sit in front of the loopers and needles and trim excess fabric from the seam edge. The stitches are then able to form over a clean finished edge for optimum effect.

The moveable knife is either recessed and attaches to the lower part of the serger near the base plate and loopers, or is attached above the base plate and loopers on an arm that cuts in a guillotine-type action. Both types of moveable knives are able to be disengaged from the cutting position. The fixed knife should be attended only by your mechanic when it requires replacing.

Please note: Neither Nancy nor I disengage the moveable knife except when we are using coverstitch or chainstitch. We are aware that some people still choose to disengage the knife for flatlock.

We prefer to teach alternative methods and use appropriate feet which come as a standard serger accessory, or are available as an optional extra, to assist in precision sewing. Our decision not to disengage the moveable knife is born out of our experience over the years: some students forget to reengage the knife and risk damaging their serger, often expensively. This is so easily prevented by selecting the appropriate foot that we choose not to go into detail about this method. I was once told by a teacher that forgetfulness and idiocy are not covered under warranty!

DIFFERENTIAL FEED

Differential Feed is one of those things "we just have to have" and to this day many people do not really understand it. While you are familiarizing yourself with your serger, take the presser foot off. Coming up through the base plate there are two sets of teeth or feed dogs. The front set is larger than the rear set, but the most important feature is that they can move independently of one another.

The differential will be set at a neutral setting straight out of the box. This may be represented as a number, typically 1, or as a letter, typically N. This means that the serger is set to do regular sewing on fabrics, such as a medium woven fabric, with threads that will not stretch or pucker and will prevent the likelihood of stitching challenges.

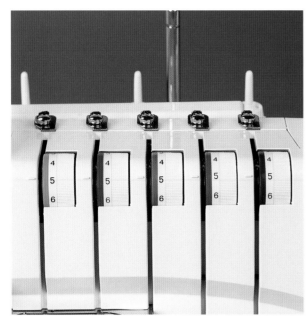

Color coded tension dials.

Simple adjustments.

Regardless of the letter or numeral, the adjustments are numbers greater than or less than 1.0, up to 2.0 or down to 0.7. Depending upon the brand of serger, the differential feed is adjusted with a dial or at the touch of a stitch selector, usually in increments of 0.1 in decimal points.

Adjusting the differential feed to a *greater number* means that fabric is being fed in to the serger at a faster rate than it comes out, pushing fullness or stretch into the fabric. With knit fabric, this increased differential rate means that the fabric is not stretched while being sewn, preventing fluted edges and creating perfectly flat seams. With woven fabric, the fullness being pushed into the fabric is represented as gathers and can vary from a gentle ease to full flounces.

Adjusting the differential feed to a number *less than the neutral setting* holds the fabric back a little, retarding its movement at the front feed dog. This puts some drag on the fabric, preventing puckers or fluting from occurring.

Individual fabrics will respond to these adjustments quite differently, but because of the small increments in adjustment that are possible, the perfect stitching solution is readily achievable.

STITCH WIDTH

Variable stitch width can be achieved in a number of ways with the versatility of your next-generation serger. The reference point for the width of a stitch is always the needle, referring to the distance from the needle to the cut edge of the fabric. The widest stitch is a 5-thread stitch with its industry finish, up to $^3/_8$ inch (9mm) wide. The widest regular stitch is the 4-thread overlock or 3-thread wide stitch, a true $^1/_4$

inch (6mm) wide at its default setting. For a narrower stitch, remove the left needle and the remaining right-hand needle becomes the reference point. On this caliber of serger, the narrowest stitch, such as a rolled hem, is achieved by retracting the stitch finger. The fixed lower blade can also be adjusted, further increasing or decreasing stitch width as required.

STITCH LENGTH

Stitch length measures the distance between the needle penetration points along the fabric, either in the seam line in an overlock stitch or in the body of the fabric with coverstitch. Some sergers have inbuilt parameters which determine the most suitable length for the stitch, the "default" setting. On most models the default length can be adjusted longer or shorter, though some individual stitches have limitations for safety reasons. Individual stitches usually have pre-set lengths which are shown on the display screen.

DISPLAY SCREEN

Many of the coverstitch sergers have information screens providing a built-in instruction book for your immediate reference. I liken this to my spare brain when I am sewing to a punishing deadline! It just makes life so easy at the serger.

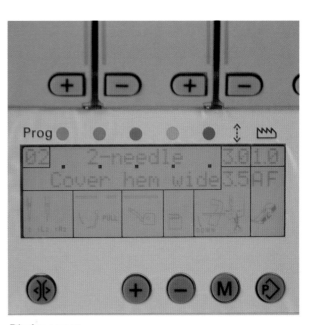

Display screen.

While there is some variation between the brands, they all highlight the appropriate information for your stitch selection: cutting width, stitch length, needle positions and differential feed ratio as soon as you key in the stitch you require. Some screens are touch activated; other screens are controlled with touch pads to access or change your stitch or information.

The display screen is an invaluable and timesaving assistant. Still your serger manual is your second best resource, and your sewing machine dealer is the very best serger resource you can have and will answer the questions Nancy and I may have had no room to address.

MEMORY

Whoever said "what you see is what you get" did not have a serger with memory. What an absolute bonus to be able to store your special stitches for use time and again! The memory is not a feature that you can see on your serger; rather it is a storage system for changes you may have made to your stitches and is invaluable when particular techniques are used regularly. It is available in many of the coverstitch sergers.

FOOT PRESSURE

Another unseen ally in serger use, adjustable foot pressure often is the feature that makes or breaks a project. Easily accessible with a dial or lever which is generally external on your serger, the simple adjustments allow you to change the pressure being exerted on your fabric. Choose lower pressure for thick winter fabrics or a little extra pressure on your lightweight fabrics.

NEEDLE REFERENCE MARKS

Raised ridges or colored lines on the front edge of your presser foot are the needle reference marks that line up with the needles to indicate just where they enter the fabric. They are an indispensable tool for stitching accuracy. There may be markings for both coverstitch and conventional serging on the one foot or there may be separate markings on a number of feet.

ROLLED HEM STITCH FINGER

The sergers in this class all have readily retractable stitch fingers for creating the popular rolled hem; refer to Stitch Width above for more detail.

FREE ARM

The free arm is a valuable tool for many applications such as sewing wristbands, neck edges and hem finishes. It comes in and out of fashion and is available on many models other than the coverstitch sergers. Those who buy a serger with a free arm specifically to sew these finishes for their baby's wristbands may be a little disappointed that the free arm is too large for their baby unless he or she is a teenager! Other techniques are more suitable for small openings.

"D" ZONE

As you look at your serger, the space between the needles and the body of the machine to the right is valuable for many coverstitch and chainstitch functions and particularly fabric manipulation. From the stitching side it is a general "D" shape, hence our name for it.

SIMPLIFIED THREADING AND COLOR CODING

The old bogey of "it's too hard to thread" has been largely dispelled with today's sergers. Color coding is standard on all this range of sergers, simple guides you can snap your thread through, molded thread paths in some

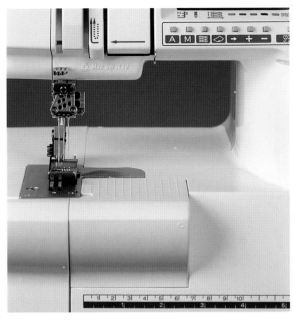

"D" Zone.

cases and much better lighting than sergers of old have simplified the entire process. Some sergers on the market have guides that are highlighted for the required thread paths, tiltable needle bars and even air threading where the thread is drawn through the guides. Nancy and I believe that any serger is easy to thread once you do it a number of times!

SAFETY FEATURES

"Bells and whistles" are a real plus at the serger, saving both mistakes and time! A variety of alarms are built in as safety features, emitting a "beep" when you try to do something outside the built-in parameters of what the serger considers typical or

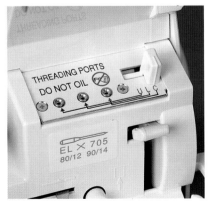

Air threading.

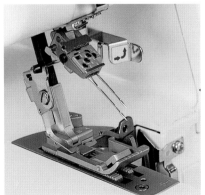

Tilt out needle clamp.

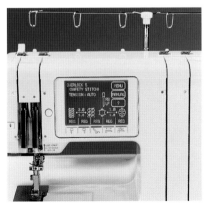

Lighted thread paths.

safe. They can vary from an alarm indicating when the front cover is open, a raised presser foot, disengaged knife or an inappropriate selection of stitch lengths for the stitch selected on some sergers. Stitch length and differential feed limitation for individual stitches can also cause the alarms to signal. They are one of the unseen bonuses that come with the new generation of sergers.

Your choice of a coverstitch serger is dictated by factors beyond Nancy's and my control. We both advocate you get the best that you can afford and follow up at your machine dealer for lessons where many basic lessons will be included free of charge with your purchase. At an extra fee, specialty lessons or classes, often with specialist sergins, such as Nancy and me, are an investment in your passion and skills development. No matter which coverstitch serger you own, learn it and you'll love it!

Serger Features

All sergers are listed in alphabetical order and met our criteria of incorporating coverstitch and chainstitch with regular serger features. While all take standard household needles, some brands specify certain needle types as the preferred option. All sergers in this category were capable of a 2, 3, 4, and 5-thread stitch as well as both coverstitch and chainstitch.

Check individual features in the close-up photos; the following lists general features of each serger within the category.

Babylock Evolve

Triple Coverstitch, small "D" section

Automatic Thread Delivery Systems

Expressive Stitches

Jet air threading, stitch up to 8 threads simultaneously

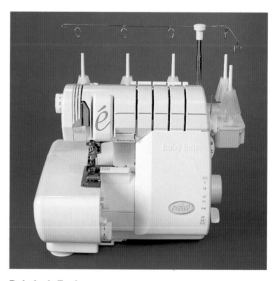

Babylock Evolve.

Bernina 1300DC

Triple Coverstitch, small "D" section

LCD Screen, programmed stitches

Manual tensions, molded thread paths, swing out presser foot

Upper knife

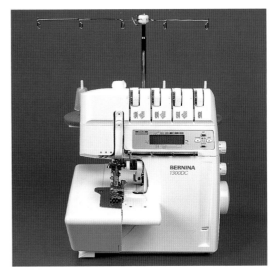

Bernina 1300 DCC.

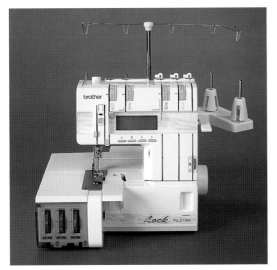

Brother PL2100.

Brother PL2100

Triple Coverstitch, medium "D" section

LCD Screen, built-in stitch guide, stitch memories

Manual tensions, all dials accessible at the front of the serger

Elna 945

Triple Coverstitch, medium "D" section

LCD Screen, programmed stitches, stitch memories

Automatic tensions, manual override

Tilt needle bar

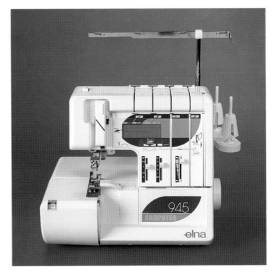

Elna 945.

Husqvarna Viking Huskylock 936

Triple Coverstitch, large "D" section

LCD Sewing Adviser, programmed stitches, stitch memories

Manual tensions

Dual lighting

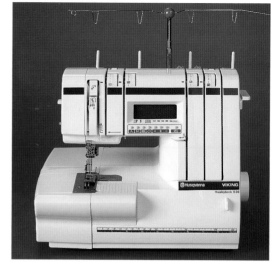

Husqvarna Viking Huskylock 936.

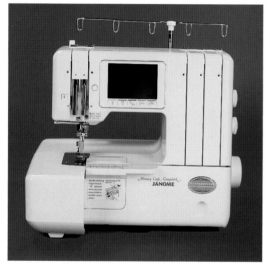

Janome Compulock 888.

Janome Compulock 888

Wide Coverstitch, large "D" section

Color Touch Screen, programmed stitches, stitch memories

Automatic tensions, manual override

Light-up diodes show thread path

Pfaff Hobbylock 4872

Triple Coverstitch, medium "D" section

LCD Screen, programmed stitches, stitch memories

Automatic tensions, manual override

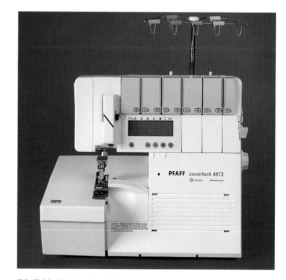

Pfaff Hobbylock 4872.

Singer Quantumlock 14T957DC

Triple Coverstitch, medium "D" section

Built-in stitch guide, color-coded thread paths

Manual tensions

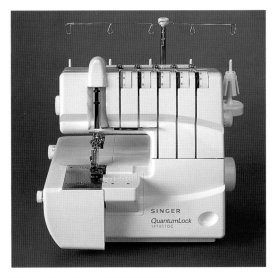

Singer Quantomlock 14T957DC.

t w o

Serger Serendipity

Why Create Using a Serger?

You might be asking yourself, why use a serger to unlock my creative talents? Why move away from the comfort zone of my sewing machine to dive into this multi-threaded, multi-needled little machine? What more can a serger provide me that my sewing machine cannot?

The answer is LOTS! There is a whole world of unique stitch formations and creative applications for them that exist only with the serger. These creative stitches and techniques are easy to learn and great fun to experiment with. To sew, on average, three times faster than most traditional household sewing machines, to form cleanly cut and finished edges in a flash, to sew unique stitch formations, to accomplish something as basic as dependable professional-looking seam edges, a serger definitely earns its place in your sewing room. Let's explore the possibilities.

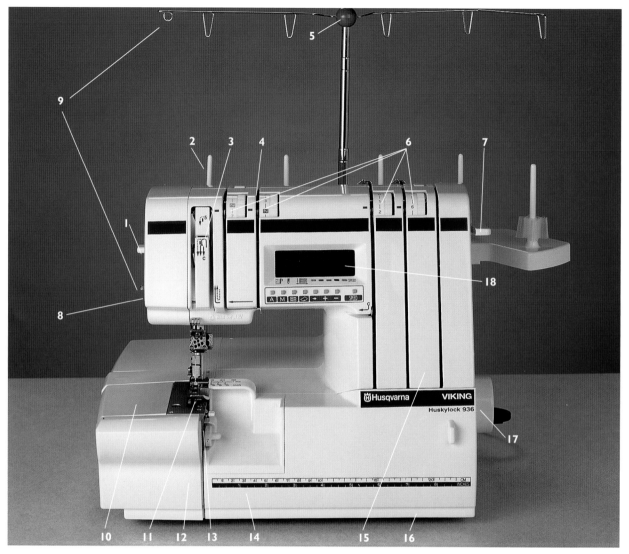

The Viking 936 serger, front cover closed. The parts labeled are: 1. Presser foot adjustment dial; 2. Spool pin; 3. Thread take-up lever cover; 4. Thread guides; 5. Telescopic thread stand; 6. Thread tension dials; 7.Presser foot lift stand; 8. Thread cutter; 9. Thread guides for decorative thread/cording; 10. Upper cutter knob; 11. Presser foot; 12.Sewing surface, flat bed cover; 13. Cutter width/stitch width adjusting dial; 14. Cutter cover; 15. Front panel; 16. Front cover; 17. Handwheel; 18. Sewing Advisor display.

PRACTICAL POSITIVES

Speed

Most sergers sew an average of 1500 spm (stitches per minute) at full out, pedal-to-the-metal speed. If you are a speed sewer you'll appreciate a machine that can give you perfect results while sewing as fast as you desire. Traditional household sewing machines do not always perform at their best at a consistent high speed, sewing skipped or broken stitches or mismatched decorative patterns. Often speed sewers are encouraged to buy heavy industrial sewing machines built for velocity. Switching to a different machine for extra fast seaming is not needed when you work with a serger— they are built to go fast! And what is the advantage of all that speed? Projects, techniques, cleanly finished beautiful edges are completed in a fraction of the time, very professionally.

Professional Results

No other machine can cleanly cut, overedge and seam fabrics together as effortlessly as a serger. Back in the early days of sewing, women who were tailoring fine garments

Inside looper, front cover open, Viking 936.

painstakingly bound each and every cut edge of a garment with bias strips of fabric before putting the project together. Even though beautiful, this tedious preassembly step was enough to discourage quantity sewing. It simply took too much time. Alternatives to binding were discouraging: pinked edges raveled, sewing machine overedging was not always "nibble free." But when using a correctly balanced stitch on the serger there is not a single fabric that cannot be successfully clean-finished suiting even the fussiest sewer.

Intentionally Rippled Seams

Ever want to create a ripply "lettuce" edge to a tee shirt, child's socks or bias cut scarf? Dial your differential feed down to have the front feed dog move more slowly than the back, creating drag. This drag will pull on the fabric as it is being serged and the serged stitches will lock that rippling effect in place. No sewing machine can easily duplicate these effects while sewing a perfectly clean finished edge.

Seams That Stretch On and On

Because of its unique needle and looper interaction, a serger can create a seam in knits that has much more stretch than anything produced by a traditional sewing machine. Every serger has specially designed stretch seams that are customized for knit seaming that make working with simple tee shirt interlock to densely knitted

Lycra to delicate swimwear easy and fun. Pair these specialized stretch seams with extra stretchy texturized nylon threads such as Wooly Nylon® and Wooly Poly, and you will see a marked difference in the quality and durability a serger knit seam can produce.

Super Strong Woven Seams

Let's not forget that sergers work wonderfully on wovens, too! With twice the needles and double the amount of thread used in the needles and loopers, a simple seam serged on a woven fabric is both strong and cleanly finished in one pass. There is no seam comparable on a sewing machine that can compete with a simple, balanced tension 4-thread overlock seam. This strong and clean seam is ideal for construction on rough and tumble kids clothes and home decorating projects. Quilters take note. A 4-thread seam is ideal for flip and sew quilt-as-you-go quilts. Joining the multiple layers of fabric and batting together with a serger seam yields a neatly compressed, flat seam. Be tempted to use it in your next quilt project—it works beautifully.

CREATIVE CONSIDERATIONS—SERGER SPECIFIC STITCHES

Rolled Hems

Beautiful and discreet rolled hem edges are easily sewn by any serger. Stitching over a narrow pin found on the base plate of the serger with tightened thread tension creates a fine rolled edge that is not easily sewn on a sewing machine. Deviate from the

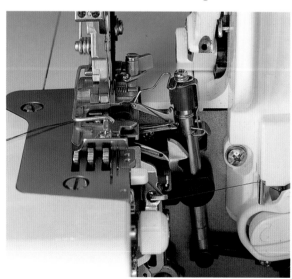

basic rolled edge by adding filler cords, fish line, fine wires, beads and decorative cords and you have a treasure chest of truly unique creative options that cannot be touched by a sewing machine.

Flatlocking Options

Where else but with a serger could you sew a reversible stitch that has two totally different appearances top and bottom and loads of creative possibilities? Achieved by disengaging the upper looper, a serger flatlock allows two pieces of fabric to be joined in a perfectly flat seam, eliminating all bulk. Flatlocked seams in polar fleece socks give the most comfortable wear.

Upper looper disengaged, converter cap installed.

Bernina 1300CC.

Flatlocking wovens allows for fiber weaving possibilities in the "ladders" part of the stitch. Want a blanket stitch on the edge of a fleece throw? Flatlocking is your stitch of choice. Flatlocking with "ladders side out" gives a hand seamed look on leathers and suede and is completely unduplicatable on a sewing machine.

Not Your Ordinary Overedging

Overlocked or overedged seams are the bread and butter stitch formations for which sergers are best known. However, given a creative tweaking with special threads, braids or elastics, these basic techniques become far from ordinary. Beautiful and heavy decorative threads too thick to pass through the eye of a sewing machine needle flow freely through the looper eyes found on a serger. Soft and cuddly edges on infant receiving blankets are no harder than overedging with fine knitting yarn or texturized wooly serger threads. Want beefier edges on your next creation? Your serger allows you to serge on top of serging, offsetting the edge and building a custom trim. Hunting for braid in a custom color? Select any heavy decorative thread, place it in both loopers and serge over a base. Want that braid to stretch? Serge over elastic for a custom trim with give.

Practical and Creative Coverstitching

Being serger enthusiasts, Anne and I were both very excited when coverstitch and chainstitch were added to the all-star serger lineup. The most unique feature of both coverstitching and chainstitching is that you are no longer restricted to sewing on the edge. Because the knife is disengaged for both these stitches, the sewer is free to travel within the body of the project, giving us many creative possibilities.

Created using a variety of needle options and a looper, coverstitching exactly duplicates the ready-to-wear hem finish found on knits. Appearing as parallel rows of straight stitching on the top and zigzags on the bottom, this stitch is reversible. By combining decorative threads on the serger in many positions, multiple creative looks can be stitched. Just flip-flopping the way your fabric is placed on the serger will allow you to duplicate exactly the garment finishes found on trendy sportswear. Many decorative possibilities for coverstitch will be discussed in later pages of this book, but suffice it to say that the possibilities are endless and unique to a serger.

Chainstitching

Like coverstitch, chainstitching is serged within the body of fabric without any cutting taking place. Having its practical applications in temporary seam basting for alterations, the chainstitch truly shines in home decorating applications. Because the "chain" part of the stitch occurs on the bottom of the fabric, there is an element of drama as you turn over your work to see the serged results. Because the lower chain is formed by a looper with a large eye, heavy decorative threads can easily be used with spectacular results. Yards and yards of chainstitch thread chains are ideal for wrapping into custom home decorating tassels, dolls' hair and garment button loops. There is absolutely no sewing machine technique that can rival a serger chainstitch.

Have we convinced you that your serger has so many creative possibilities? Combine speed with cleanly sewn edges, unique stitches and a whole world of threads, techniques and possibilities and you have some of the many of the reasons why Anne and I definitely choose our sergers as much needed and much loved creative powerhouses in our sewing rooms! We hope to entice you even more on the following pages.

Helping Hands

You may ask just why you need to consider some of these extras at your serger. The answer is easy: they make your life a lot simpler! Playing with texture, dimension and different techniques make some of these seemingly odd items a perfect addition to your cache of must-have tools.

NEEDLES

The ultimate companion to great threads is the correct needle. There are sizes and types to suit multiple purposes to consider in selecting your needle. Refer to your manual for the correct system for your serger and remember that most sergers are calibrated to a #90 needle. Always change the needles after a maximum of six hours of serging: your serger runs at a much faster speed than your sewing machine, requiring more regular replacement. The nurse in me also asks that you dispose of them safely, please, in a rigid container.

STABILIZERS

Throughout our projects you will see liberal usage of some nontraditional products in the serger process. Opening your mind to the "what-if" thought process leads you to experiment with items that you may have thought only useable for sewing and embroidery. We encourage you to stock your serger workroom with a variety of these products to help make your creative process easier, more intriguing and just plain fun!

Water Soluble Stabilizers

There are many brands on the market, most generally considered a product for machine embroidery. Try placing a strip of water-soluble stabilizer on top of your fabric as you stitch any edges where thread fibers may show, notably a rolled hem. The stabilizer rolls with the fabric to prevent "pokies" and is removed with water at a later stage. Water-soluble stabilizers also simplify working blanket stitch edging on your serger projects. The stabilizer provides a base for the stitch formation and is easily removed upon completion.

Stabilizers.

The opaque paper water soluble sheets are another great product for serger use: place a piece under any coverstitch work with fine fabrics and not a pucker will be in site. This stabilizer is usually removed with a gentle tug after the needle perforates the paper. Any remaining product washes away.

Water Soluble Adhesive Stabilizer (Aqua Bond)

Relatively new in the U.S. marketplace, this product is a hybrid of a traditional water soluble stabilizer and self-adhesive paper. Currently sold in 1-yard packages, this stabilizer has a top release paper which, when removed, exposes a sticky surface. Decorative threads, yarns and fibers can be patted and held in place on this sticky surface. A layer of traditional, film-type water soluble stabilizer is placed on top of the sticky product. The whole stabilizer/fiber unit is taken to the serger and stitched through. All stabilizers are then dissolved in water with repeated rinsings. Truly a fascinating process, it allows you literally to sew on thin air and create your own fabric!

Temporary Fabric Adhesive Spray

There are many brands on the market, some fabric specific, others multi-purpose. A light mist of spray holds two pieces of fabric together for a multitude of purposes such as garment or quilt piecing, quilting and appliqué. A water soluble glue stick is sometimes a suitable substitute for small areas. Temporary adhesives are a wonderful substitute for pins!

Spray On Fusible Web

Replace traditional paper-backed web with this fusible product and you will forever eliminate the sticky residue that oftentimes occurs when using an iron. This "web in a can" is sprayed on the wrong side of fabric, allowed to dry, and then fused to another fabric with a dry iron. The bond is clean and strong. I auditioned this product when creating the serger tassel in the Home Decorating section of the book (Chapter 8) and love it.

Threads.

THREADS

We both love beautiful threads and anyone who creatively serges should have a steadily growing stash in the studio. Because the serger's loopers have such large eyes, we are able to use a much larger variety of thread products than sewing machine owners. Serging showcases beautiful threads wonderfully with its unique stitch formations. We give all our readers carte blanche to buy each and every spool that calls to you.

Listed below are some of the thread types used in this book.

All-Purpose Threads (upper right hand corner)

These are the workhorses in your serger thread cabinet. Serger cone and spooled threads can be used decoratively or hidden in construction seaming. Look for and buy the best thread quality you can afford. The serger thread should be smooth with no lumps or irregularities. It should not snap easily when pulled. Cones last a long time, so consider your purchase a long term investment. Spooled thread used in your sewing machine can also be successfully used on a serger. Assure that the top of the spool is smooth with no slotted edges to catch the thread as it feeds into the serger. Lastly, always have a cone or two of texturized nylon or polyester thread on hand, such as Wooly Nylon by YLI or WoolyPoly by Superior Threads. These threads are uniquely stretchy and ideal for serging seams with "give " for knits and swimwear. No other traditional thread type will give you as much stretch as these specialty threads.

Sparklers—Metallics (lower right hand corner)

Just as in sewing, metallics can add excitement to serging. Both spooled and cone thread put ups work well in the serger. Always use a needle designed for metallics if using the metallics in the needle. As with your sewing machine, serge at a decreased speed to avoid thread breakage. Some of our favorites are Halo by Superior Threads, Yenmet by OESD (both are on cones), and Sulky and Madeira spooled polyester core metal-wrapped fibers.

Thicker Decorative Threads (lower left hand corner)

Try heavy machine embellishment threads which are much thicker than regular threads and give a rich finish. Some of the new machine quilting and embroidery cottons, in delicate or bold variegations, add subtle elegance to projects, while the glitzy threads add funky pizzazz to any project. Solid colors, variegated and textured threads, crochet cottons, hand-dyed threads . . . there seems to be a proliferation of threads erupting in the market adding to the palette of the embellishment artist.

Don't overlook the quietly elegant threads on the market today. Subtly colored or beautifully texturized, these threads can take your serged stitches to an elegant level. Wonderfully variegated and solid 12 wt. cottons such as Blendables by Sulky, Cordonnet by Mettler or Jeans Stitch by YLI blend beautifully with their matte finishes. Monet by YLI is a wool cone thread that duplicates a knitted edging when serged. Because the eyes of the loopers are large, the world of heavy threads and fabulous texture is only a practice away. Be prepared to experiment; just be aware that some threads have the potential to cause you to become a serious threadaholic. We both love and regularly work with heavier threads such as Pearl Crown Rayon and Designer 6 from YLI for more pronounced decorative effects.

Embroidery Threads (upper left hand corner)

Indulge yourself in a rainbow of color serging with this thread group. We love and liberally use embroidery threads in all weights and fabrications. From hand-dyed cottons to factory variegated gradations and everything in between, these threads make your serging sing. Liberal use of them in art pieces is a must. Use of them in simple edgings is a joy.

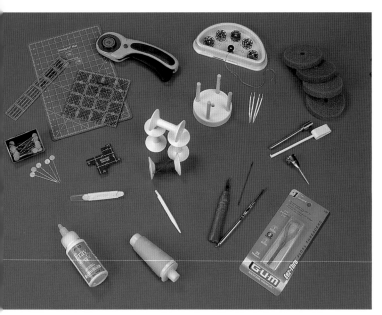

Accessories.

OTHER ACCESSORIES

Horizontal Spool Pins

These are indispensable for feeding any flat ribbon-like threads at the serger; the horizontal pin attaches to either of the looper spool pins. The thread or fiber winds off smoothly and evenly, minimizing twisting and breaking. Wonderful for hologram threads, flat ribbons, and floss-like threads.

Thread Palette

A round platform with a central hole that sits over either of the looper spool pins, the Thread Palette has an additional four spool holders. A must for fiber artists, this is fabulous for thread blending and when rich texture is preferred.

EZ Winder™ Thread Spools

The EZ Winders™ are over-sized plastic spools which attach with an adaptor to the sewing machine bobbin winder for those threads that do not come on regular cones. Wind these specialty threads slowly at the machine and they will then sit comfortably on either of the looper spool pins, another must for the embellishment artist.

Adaptor Pins

These adaptors keep your spools from wobbling on your spool pin, eliminating thread cone holders and allowing your thread to feed smoothly. The Master Pin™ fits all sewing machines with a vertical spool holder, allowing your cone thread to sit snugly over the spindle.

Thread Cushions

These flat circular foam pads sit under thread spools. They hold the thread spool more securely in place and you can use most cone or regular spools with them. They are great when you are using regular spools, especially with embroidery threads as they stop the thread from "puddling" under the spool. The other practical advantage is that you have somewhere to put the needles you are not using.

Bobbin Mate™

A semi-circular platform with cover which holds up to five sewing machine bobbins, the Bobbin Mate is indispensable when you need to match your thread and fabric but serger cone thread is unavailable in the right color. Wind a bobbin for each of the thread paths you require, feed them through the opening in the clear cover and off you sew.

Trolley Needle

The trolley needle sits over the end of your index finger like a thimble and has a blunt needle-like extension. This is terrific for holding tricky fibers or materials in place at the serger. The advantage of the trolley needle is that it frees up your hands because it is already in place on your index finger.

Dental Floss Threaders

Yes, we mean the floss threaders that you buy at the drugstore or supermarket! These flexible tools have a large loop, perfect to slip threads that ravel through and then to feed through the eye of the looper with the rigid extension arm. The floss threader is also perfect for textured nylon because the blue color makes them easier to see for some applications than the fine filament wire threaders that are available.

Needle Inserters

This nifty device is a lifesaver at times! It holds your needle while you insert (or remove) it for any needle position. Available in a variety of styles, some also have a brush on one end. There is no such thing as too many if it means no more needles lost in the body of the serger.

Double Eyed Needles

Very useful for short or long thread tails, the eye is large enough to accommodate a number of threads, which allows you to take your serger chain tails back along the row of stitching. Couple the large eye with a blunt tipped needle and they will find many uses in your sewing repertoire.

Pins

Deadheading pins at your serger is another technique that is not covered under warranty!

If you need to pin any fabrics together for sewing, use flower head pins so that the foot can glide over the top with the pin parallel, not perpendicular, to the fabric edge. Alternatively, use some of the huge array of temporary adhesives that are on the market or the chainstitch as a basting stitch, which will pull out in a heartbeat!

Seam Gauge

Small and handy, they ensure you have an accurate seam at any time. If you are a quilter, check out the 4-thread overlock and narrow 5-thread stitch for a true $^1/_4$ in (6mm) stitch. Nancy and I both know already that you can quilt accurately at the serger, but just show your friends for an "I told you so" moment.

Liquid Seam Sealants

There are numerous brands of chemical sealant on the market. They permanently seal the ends of fibers which would otherwise ravel. Tip a small amount onto a nonporous surface like a saucer and dip a pin or dental brush pick into it. Use the point of the pin or the tiny brush from the dental pick to apply a fine line of sealant to the ends of thread tails or in places where the threads may start unraveling unless secured.

To keep the seam or area to be treated pliable, use an appliqué mat, sandwiching the area between two layers and press while still wet.

Brush Picks

A dental hygiene product that is terrific for use with fabric sealants, the brush pick has a small brush at one end and a point at the other. Apply a thin line of your liquid seam sealant from the point or the brush; the brush holds more liquid and is better for a larger project or area, the point perfect for fine detailed areas.

Reverse Serging Instrument (aka Seam Ripper)

Yes, sadly there are times when our passion carries us away and we have to reverse the error we have made! Invest in a few seam rippers at a time because the blades do not stay sharp forever. I am a registered nurse by profession (a sergin' by choice), trust me, it's true. I also believe a sharp instrument is much safer than a blunt instrument since you do not have to hack to undo any stitching and possibly create unwittingly even more creative opportunities.

Chocolate Cache

An absolute "must" for those times when you need a break. Or whenever. Need I say more?

three

Serger Tapas

WE FELT THAT IT WAS only fitting to include a sense of the location where this book idea was born—over a wonderful meal in a Spanish restaurant accompanied by homemade sangria. As we nibbled delicious Spanish "tapas," little meals, we hashed out the details of the book on a napkin. This allusion to our momentus lunch is especially appropriate for our serger technique section. We think of these stitch formations as tasty bits of serger joy, much like our meal.

This chapter is meant to be the technical "how-to" reference for the book. Stitch formations are explained, machine movements demystified, and special tips shared to help you serge as creatively as possible. Take time to serge small samples of each technique, noting your specific serger's preference as to stitch length, tensions, and special adjustments. Specific numbers on tensions are purposely not given since most brands of sergers have their own mechanical personalities. Refer to your owner's guidebook for the stepping off point for these stitches. Then, tweak them as needed for the desired result. Serging is all about fearlessly experimenting and having discovered creative options not found on our sewing machines. Enjoy the journey and Buen Apetito!

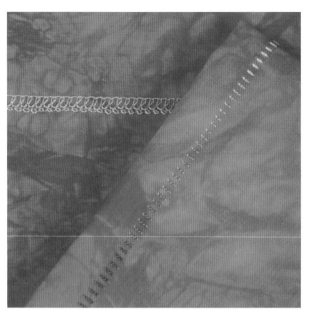

3-thread flatlock.

3-THREAD FLATLOCK
(2 thread option also available)

Flatlocking is a stitch unique to the serger. It is designed to join 2 pieces of fabric together, pulling the seam on each side to flatten the stitches. It is a bulk-free seam. Needle tension is always extremely loose because this is the part of the stitch that will give the extra room to allow the fabrics to flatten. A 3-thread flatlock, 1 needle and both loopers, will be a more secure seam in stress areas. A 2-thread flatlock, 1 needle and lower looper only, will pull more flatly because of one less thread in the seam. On both variations there will be two distinct sides. One side will show "ladders" only, the vertically straightened needle stitches. The opposite side will show a more traditional looking overlock seam.

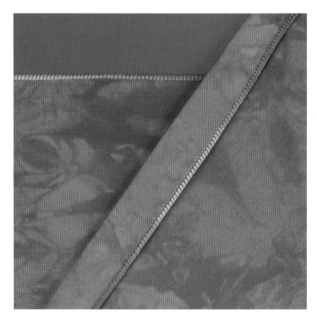

3-thread narrow rolled hem.

3-THREAD NARROW ROLLED HEM
(2-Thread option also available)

Probably one of the most popular serger stitches, a narrow rolled hem produces a fine rolled edge. The right needle is used with both loopers. The tension on the lower looper is considerably tightened to pull the fabric and thread into a tunnel. Beautiful results can be had by placing decorative threads in the upper looper position. A 2-thread rolled hem can also be serged using the right needle and lower looper only. The resulting hem edge is less thread-heavy and is especially appropriate for sheer fabrics.

Chainstitch basting.

CHAINSTITCH BASTING SEAM

Chainstitch is another stitch formation that is exclusive to a serger. Sewn using a needle and looper for chainstitching, this stitch has practical beginnings. Its primary application is for temporary basting in home decorating or garment projects. A chainstitch basted seam can be quickly removed by pulling on the looper thread at the *end* of the seam.

Decorative chainstitching.

DECORATIVE CHAINSTITCHING

Because the eye of the looper is large, heavy decorative threads can be used with chainstitching. This is an unusually dramatic way to sew since you will serge with the wrong side of the fabric facing up while the decorative part of the stitch forms on the wrong side. Until you serge and turn the fabric over, you really do not know what you have. Remember to increase your stitch length appropriately as you increase your decorative thread width. This will allow the threads to lie smoothly and avoid bunching.

CHAINSTITCH SMOCKING—STABLE

Simple chainstitching can be turned into puffy smocking simply be increasing your differential feed setting. As the serge pushes more fabric into the needles, tiny pleats are caught in the stitch formation. This technique works best with lightweight fabrics and rows spaced $1/2$ inch (1cm) apart or less. Always allow for extra fabric to accommodate the fullness taken up by the gathering.

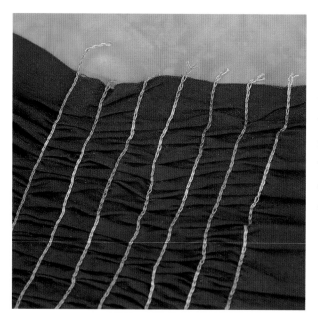

Chainstitch smocking—stable.

CHAINSTITCH SMOCKING— STRETCH

Changing the chainstitch thread to a fine spooled elastic thread allows the serger to sew smocking with give. Your differential feed setting is increased so that fabric is already slightly gathered as the tucks are being secured with the elastic thread. The magic happens after the serging is finished. Take your elastic smocked yardage to a steam iron. Hold the iron slightly above the smocking and watch the elastic fibers draw up before your eyes. Tug on the gathers to straighten them while still warm from the iron.

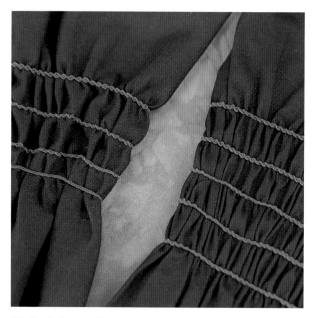

Chainstitch smocking—stretch.

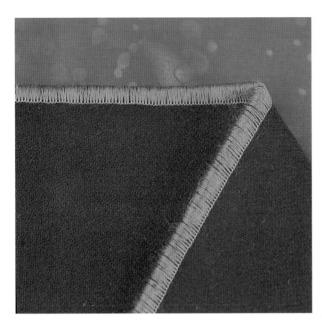

2-thread wrapped edge.

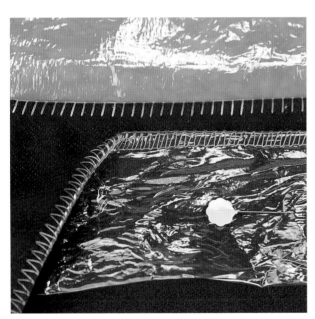

2-thread blanket stitch.

2-THREAD WRAPPED EDGE

If you are short 1 spool of decorative thread and still want to try to create a serged edge, this technique is for you. Use one needle (left or right) and the lower looper. Thread the lower looper with the decorative thread and the needle with all-purpose thread. Extremely loose lower looper tension will draw the loops from the front to the back and encase the edge. It's a great thread saver with professional results.

2-THREAD BLANKET STITCH

This is one of my favorite stitches that cannot be duplicated in any way on the sewing machine. Appearing difficult, it actually is quite simple.

- **Set serger for a 2-thread flatlock.**

- **On a finished edge, pin a double thick piece of water soluble stabilizer. Extend the stabilizer ¹/₂ inch (1cm) past the finished edge. The larger piece of the stabilizer should remain on the body of the fabric.**

- **Serge a flatlock through all layers, cutting off the small extension of stabilizer.**

- **Pull the larger stabilizer piece in the direction of the finished edge. The needle stitches will pull into a completely horizontal position to look like ladders. This is the blanket stitch. The loopers will disappear on the wrong side.**

- **Carefully remove the excess stabilizer from the finished edge or soak in water to dissolve. This is a wonderful edge finish on garments, polar fleece throws and especially attractive with variegated thread in the needle to produce color-changing "ladders."**

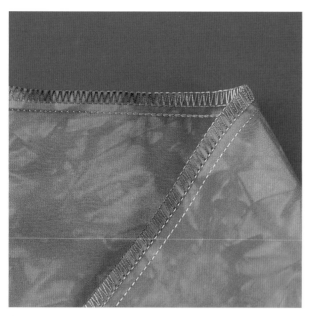

5-thread overlock—conventional.

5-THREAD OVERLOCK: CONVENTIONAL

The 5-thread stitch is formed with both the chain looper and chain needle forming the straight stitch; the upper and lower loopers and left needle form the overedge stitch simultaneously. The stitch width can be up to $3/8$ inch (9mm) wide depending upon the brand of serger you own.

This stitch is typically considered as the "industry" finish with a durable chain stitch seam and clean edge finish meeting industry and, now domestic, standards. This combination is most readily identified as the strong seam finish on the inside of jeans or sturdy ready-to-wear garments.

5-thread overlock—narrow.

5-THREAD OVERLOCK: NARROW

The stitch formation is identical to the conventional 5-thread overlock setup except the stitch finger is retracted to the rolled hem position creating a much narrower stitch. This setup yields a typical $1/4$-inch (6mm) wide stitch, perfect for quilting and seam finishes on finer or sheer ready-to-wear garments. It is often used as an external garment finish.

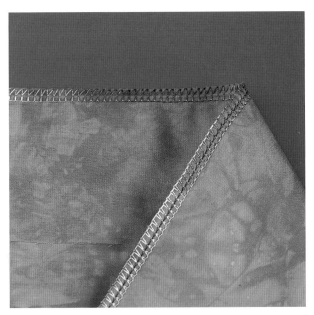

4-thread overlock.

4-THREAD OVERLOCK STITCH

A "balanced" 4-thread overlock seam is the benchmark for all other stitches: it is the most commonly used stitch. The upper and lower loopers and needles all interlock to form the stitch along the edge of the fabric. The needle threads hold, or "lock" the looper threads in position as the loopers are crossing each other. The knives are both engaged, trimming excess fabric in front of the loopers and needles to provide a clean edge over which the stitches form.

The cutting width can be adjusted to accommodate thicker or finer fabrics. This strong and clean seam is ideal for construction on children's clothes, home decorating projects, or any item requiring a very durable finish.

Wide coverstitch.

WIDE COVERSTITCH

The coverstitch is the traditional hem finish on knit garments. On the top of the fabric the stitch appears as parallel rows of stitching, while the underside appears as a zigzag. Either side may be considered as the right side of the fabric depending upon the intended function or look desired. The most unique feature of coverstitch is that you are no longer restricted to sewing along an edge.

Wide placement of needles results in a coverstitch formation usually about $1/4$ inch (6mm) in width depending upon your serger.

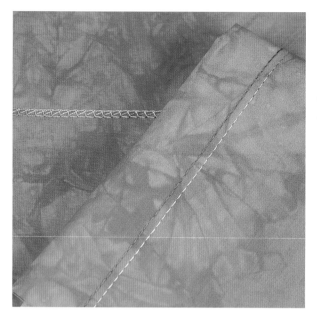

Narrow coverstitch.

NARROW COVERSTITCH

The same formation as wide coverstitch, except the stitch width is about $1/8$ inch (3mm) wide. Not all coverstitch sergers have the necessary needle positions to perform the narrow coverstitch.

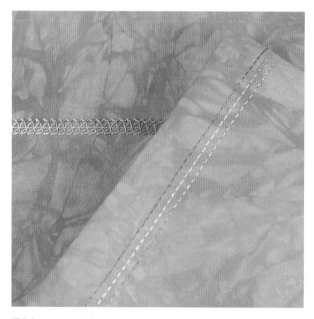

Triple coverstitch.

TRIPLE COVERSTITCH

Again, the stitch formation is the same as for wide and narrow coverstitch, this time with three needle positions allowing for three parallel rows of stitching. This setup can also convert to wide and narrow coverstitch. It is often seen on designer garments, up-market ready-to-wear as well as the edge finish of choice on pricier gym and swim wear.

Serger piping.

SERGER PIPING

- Snap piping foot onto serger.

- Cut piping cord the finished length required, plus 4 inches (10cm).

- Fold fabric strip, wrong sides together, over the cord along the long sides, notching cord under piping foot.

- Ensure the cord is sitting securely in the cording groove, raw edges of fabric facing towards cutting blade: secure with a few stitches to hold the cord stable.

- Overlock the length of fabric, slowing down a little at fabric joins.

3-thread overlock fabric making.

3-THREAD OVERLOCK FABRIC

You can use your serger to create your own fabric with the following method. The first two rows of stitching create the foundation and form the basis of the fabric. The stitches themselves form the fabric.

Method

- Cut several narrow strips of water soluble stabilizer.

- Raise the presser foot.

- Place the righthand side of a strip of water soluble stabilizer under the presser foot.

- Lower the presser foot.

- Stitch on the water soluble stabilizer for the length of the strip, cutting a sliver off as you go.

- Run the chain off the end of the stabilizer for 2 inches (5cm).

- Working from the same side, rotate the piece so that the stitching is to the left and the stabilizer is to the right.

- To stitch the next row, the left needle should enter just the outer edge of the previous row of stitching, covering a $1/4$ inch (6mm), or less, of the stitching.

- The water soluble stabilizer will be trimmed off with this row of stitching.

- Place a new strip of water soluble stabilizer with the right edge under the presser foot.

- Stitch on the water soluble stabilizer for the length of the strip, again cutting a sliver off as you go.

- Flip the water soluble stabilizer upside down so that the stitching is on the left and the strip of water soluble stabilizer is underneath and on the right.

- Stitch on the water soluble stabilizer for the length of the strip, trimming all excess.

- Continue in this manner until you have a length of serger fabric suitable for your needs.

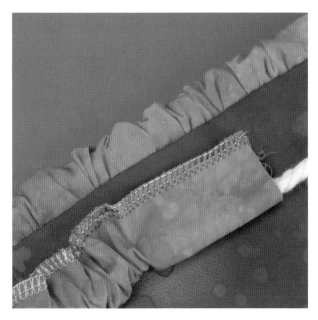

Ruched piping.

RUCHED PIPING

- Cut two strips contrasting fabric twice the length of the piping cord: measure loosely around cord and add 1 inch (2.5cm) to determine the width you need to cut your strips. Stitch fabric and cord together at one end to anchor the cord.

- Serge a balanced 4-thread stitch along both raw edges, wrong sides together, leaving the last 4 inches (10cm) open. Ease the excess fabric over the cord, distributing evenly.

- Sandwich between front and back of cushion and stitch at the sewing machine using either a buttonhole or edge-joining foot, stopping when within the last 6 inches (15cm). Overlap the open fabric end over the cord-covered fabric, folding back about $\frac{1}{4}$ inch (6mm) along the narrow end and stitch in the seam to complete the pillow top. Slip-stitch the folded edge to finish.

WIDE COVERSTITCH GATHERING

- Set the serger for coverstitch wide.

- Place your fabric under the serger presser foot; center the area to be gathered directly under the foot

- Adjust the differential feed to the maximum setting and the stitch length to the greatest number for the maximum gathering possible.

- Gather the length of the strip: adjust either or both the differential feed and the stitch length to attain your desired degree of fullness.

Wide coverstitch gathering.

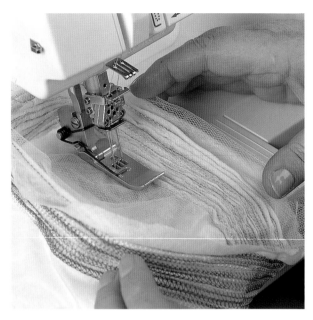

Coverstitch fabric.

COVERSTITCH FABRIC

Coverstitch fabric may be made with fine bridal tulle as a base: this method is recommended for garments where the area may be under stress at times. Omit the tulle if it is not required.

Method—Serging "In The Round"

- Place tulle and water soluble stabilizer strips together.

- Place tulle underneath, next to the feed dogs of the serger.

- Line up the serger foot along the edge of the tulle and stabilizer.

- Starting at the right side outer edge, begin stitching the long side of the strips.

- Continue until 8 inches (20cm) from the end of the strip.

- Bring the beginning short edge of the strip to where you are stitching.

- Line up both short edges and overlap them.

- Continue stitching; you will return to the starting position and will have formed a circle.

- Slightly offset your stitching by having the right needle enter the left side of the previous row of stitching.

- The needle should be covering a scant amount of the previous row of stitching.

- Continue to stitch "in the round" until you end up at the far left side of both your tulle and stabilizer.

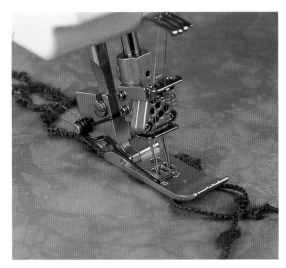

Coverstitch cable.

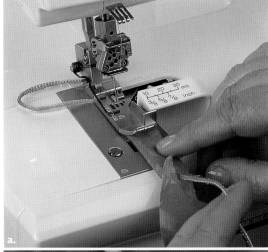

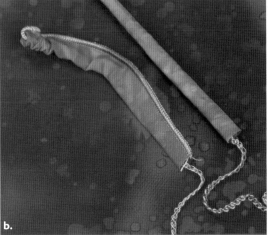

COVERSTITCH CABLE

- Set the serger for coverstitch wide.

- Cut two lengths of cord or yarn for embellishment, the length of the area to be embellished plus one third. Align them each side of the presser foot and pin in place with flower-head pins, ensuring the point of the pin is facing to the back of the presser foot. Serge slowly, taking 6 stitches only: stop with the needles lowered into the fabric and cross the cords in front of the presser foot. Stitch 6 more stitches and cross the threads in front of the presser foot once more, creating the first of your cables. Continue until finished.

SERGER ROULEAU (CORDING)

- Cut the fabric strip 1 inch (2.5cm) wider than the desired finished width.

- Serge a rolled hem thread chain about 6 inches (15cm) longer than the length of rouleau you require.

- Fold the fabric around the thread chain.

- Serge down the raw edges, trimming away about $1/2$ inch (1cm) of excess fabric, creating a tube.

- Gently pull the chain to turn the rouleau inside out.

a. Creating serger rouleau. b. Turning and finished serger rouleau.

four

Check It Out

BOTH OF US HAVE BEEN experimenting from the early serger days when this little machine was first made available to the home market. Taking to the machine
immediately, we both experimented with the techniques that our dealers and guide-
books taught us, voraciously read printed materials for additional information and
wanted more. Well, with the addition of coverstitch and chainstitch to sergers, we
got our wish. In practical applications, coverstitch allowed us to duplicate perfectly
ready-to-wear hem finishes in a flash. Chainstitch allowed easy-to-remove temporary basting for garment and home decorating projects. After we learned the practical side to the stitches, our inquisitive natures took over. Decorative cover and chain
are now two of our most enjoyable and experiment-friendly places to work on the
serger. We hope that you think so too.

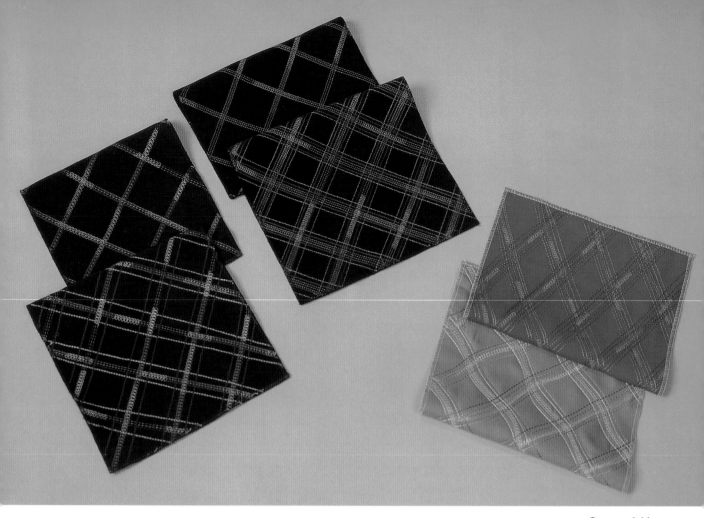

Nancy's Coverstitch Plaid

I really enjoyed the challenge of turning plain humble fabric into something really special by using the coverstitch and chainstitch formations found on my serger. By stitching intersecting rows of both stitches, I was able to fashion a custom plaid that was unlike anything available anywhere. Because of the anatomy of cover and chain-stitch formations, this plaid cannot be duplicated by a sewing machine.

This is a high drama technique. Because both the cover and chainstitches are formed on the bottom, you must place fabrics right sides down. You will see only the needle stitches until you turn the fabric over to see the beauty of the coverstitch and chains. Talk about exciting! Again, this is a very simple technique for you to enjoy, made spectacular by the availability of specialty stitches and wonderful decorative threads.

Blue denim—upper swatch—coverstitch rows only—in progress

Lower swatch—cover and chain rows—completed plaid

Threads: YLI Jeans Stitch and Pearl Crown Rayon

Black twill—upper swatch - coverstitch rows only

Lower swatch—cover and chain rows—completed plaid

Threads: Sulky 30, 35 and 40 wt. embroidery threads

Magenta wool—Angle for the intersecting lines was changed from 90 degrees to 30 degrees.

Threads: Halo by Superior Threads

Taupe twill—cover and chain lines were sewn in wavy, almost free motion.

Threads: Embroidery-weight threads in solids and variegated colors

NOTE: The plaided fabric was used on The Sahara Vest #1025 by Purrfection Artistic Wearables

DIRECTIONS

- Set your serger for a 2- or 3-needle coverstitch. Place a variegated decorative thread in the coverstitch looper. All-purpose or embroidery-weight threads can be in all needle positions.

- On the wrong side of your fabric, mark in your intersecting plaid lines with dressmaker's chalk.

- Place your marked fabric under the presser foot, wrong side facing up.

- Coverstitch on all marked rows.

- Reset your serger for a chainstitch with decorative thread in the chainstitch looper.

- Place the fabric wrong side facing up.

Chalk mark plaid lines on the wrong side of the fabric.

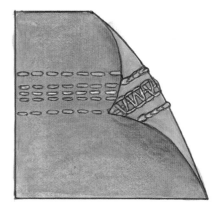

- Using your coverstitch lines as a guide, chainstitch framing rows of stitches above and below the coverstitch. Chainstitch one or two rows to frame each side of the coverstitch lines.

- Press the finished plaid. Use the yardage as an accent fabric in your next project.

Coverstitch marked lines first, then chainstitch close to the coverstitching to create "plaid."

MIX IT UP!

Coverstitch Design Fun

Once you have completed your first piece of serger plaid, experiment with some of these variations to see what you can create.

- Change the angle of the intersecting lines.

- Serge wavy lines instead of straight.

- Serge on irregularly spaced lines for a funky plaid.

- Plaid in neutral colors for a subtle look.

- Change the weights and textures of your threads in looper threads for visual and tactile variety.

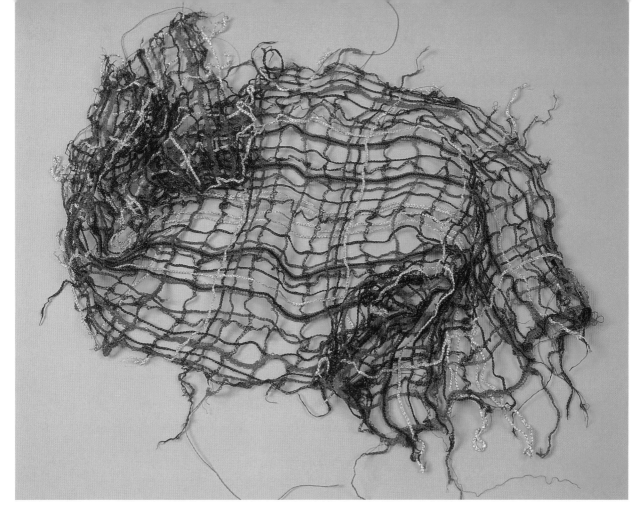

Fabric scarf—Anne.

Anne's Easy Peasy Plaid Scarf

Fabulous threads and the latest in technology have brought about the opportunity to play with the serger as never before. Threads are my tools of trade and coupled with the magic of water soluble stabilizers, making my own fabric has become one of my favorite pastimes. A word to the unwary: any form of fabric-making is seriously addictive!

MATERIALS

A variety of threads for embellishment including heavy and glitzy threads and embroidery threads (see below for actual threads used).

Water soluble stabilizer cut to slightly larger than the finished size of your scarf.

DIRECTIONS

- Work lengthwise and crosswise grids of wide coverstitch on your water soluble stabilizer.

- Work lengthwise and crosswise grids of narrow coverstitch in between the rows of wide coverstitch.

- Work lengthwise and crosswise grids of chainstitch in between the rows of wide and narrow coverstitch. Also work rows of chainstitch down the center of the wide coverstitch.

- Vary the grid so it is asymmetrical and play with different combinations of effects.

- When you have completed the stitching, immerse the scarf in cool water. Leave for a few minutes before swishing around in the water. Repeat as many times as necessary to remove the stabilizer. You will have loose scrappy fringed ends, very funky look: seal the ends with a drop of liquid seam sealant if a little more unraveling is not to your liking; otherwise leave them as is.

If you would like to add more "bling" and some really artistic elements to your scarf, leave the water-soluble stabilizer in place. Use your sewing machine to appliqué simple designs directly onto your scarf. If you have an embroidery machine, select one of your automatic appliqué designs or a design that is not too dense, and again stitch directly onto the stabilized scarf. Refer to the embroidery and techniques used in the quilt "Out of the Blue" for further design ideas. Once you have embellished your scarf, rinse as directed above.

Wide coverstitch with **YLI Candlelight**™ in the chain looper, regular cone thread in the needle.

Narrow coverstitch with **YLI Candlelight**™ in the chain looper, regular cone thread in the needle.

Chain stitch with either **YLI Designer 6**™ or **YLI Candlelight**™ in the chain looper.

Narrow coverstitch with polyester embroidery thread in the needles and a contrasting color in the chain looper.

f i v e

Inside Out and Upside Down

O NE OF THE MOST ATTRACTIVE features of the serger are the cleanly cut and wonderfully overcast edge finishes created by simple overlock stitches. Many a serger has been sold based on the wonder of seeing a blade cutting through fabric and encasing it with thread before there is any chance of it fraying. We set out to prove just how presentable the serger finishes were by designing garments that had their facings and hems on the outside. Upon close inspection, the hem allowance bands look like applied pieces to the garment, not inside-out folds. This is a great way to work with a pattern, using the pre-drawn facing and hems as design elements. The work has already been done for you. Consider cutting facings out of contrasting fabric and serging them on from the wrong side and flipping them to the right side. It's a fun look that is hardly any work at all.

Nancy's Thai Coat

To be honest, I had never sewn or worn a coat as long as this before. Anne kept insisting that we needed a duster-length garment to add balance and interest to the garment set. Trying to be open-minded, I agreed and was pleasantly surprised with the results. Even though a lightweight wool like the one Anne was using was not a practical option for my cold Chicago weather, I thought that the coat would be great in linen as a spring and summer piece. When it was finished I was glad that I gave in to Anne's insistence and plan on serging several more!

MATERIALS

Sewing Workshop Thai Coat™ pattern.

Cotton/polyester linen—yardage as indicated on the pattern envelope.

Threads for decorative chainstitching, hems, and edges.

Variations by YLI—cotton embroidery-weight thread.

Designer 6 by YLI—heavyweight untwisted rayon.

Taupe 100-percent polyester embroidery thread by OESD.

DIRECTIONS

- Cut the coat, following the pattern directions.

- Mark the hem allowances on the coat body, sleeves and overlay.

- Press the hem allowances to the garment right side to show the area available for embellishment.

- Set the serger for a narrow rolled hem with decorative thread in the upper looper.

- Finish all lower hem edges with a rolled hem.

- Reset the serger for decorative chainstitching. Place various decorative threads in the chainstitch looper. All-purpose serger thread is placed in the needle.

- Place the hem allowance right side down on the serger. Chainstitch wavy lines using decorative threads. Fill the hem allowances and facings with multiple rows in several colors.

- Construct the coat following the pattern directions.

- Using a sewing machine, edgestitch the hem allowances in place.

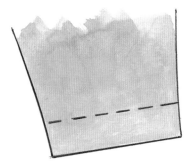

Mark hem allowances and facings to give a visual area for chainstitch detail.

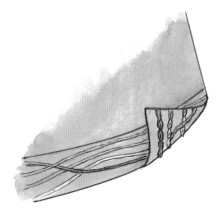

Wrong side facing up, chainstitch multiple wavy lines to add detail to the marked hem and facing areas.

"Chewing Gum" Top

On one of our past fabric forays, Anne and I found this odd piece of fabric in the designer room. We didn't know much about it except that it was from Italy, had "miscellaneous" fibers and it stretched. It was so odd that we both had to have it. When Anne returned home her daughter thought that the wrong side of the fabric looked like a piece of gum that had been stepped on—hence the garment name.

This top purposely features exposed serging to prove how clean and presentable a seam allowance is sewn with a serger. I was delighted to realize that it was the perfect color complement to my chainstitching on the coat.

MATERIALS

Vogue #7799—View A

Yardage of knit fabric as indicated on the pattern guidesheet.

DIRECTIONS

- **Cut pattern pieces following the pattern directions.**

- **Set serger for a wide, 3-thread overlock with all-purpose serger thread in all positions.**

- **Serge-seam the garment together following the directions.**

- **Eliminate the hem allowance by simply serging across the bottom of the garment. The serged hem will be very clean and bulk free.**

- **When completed, fold down the collar to expose the wrong side of the fabric and serger seams.**

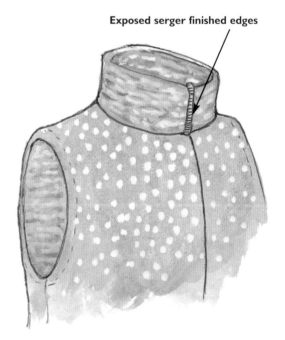

Exposed serger finished edges

Exposed serger finished edges give a boutique look to a simple top.

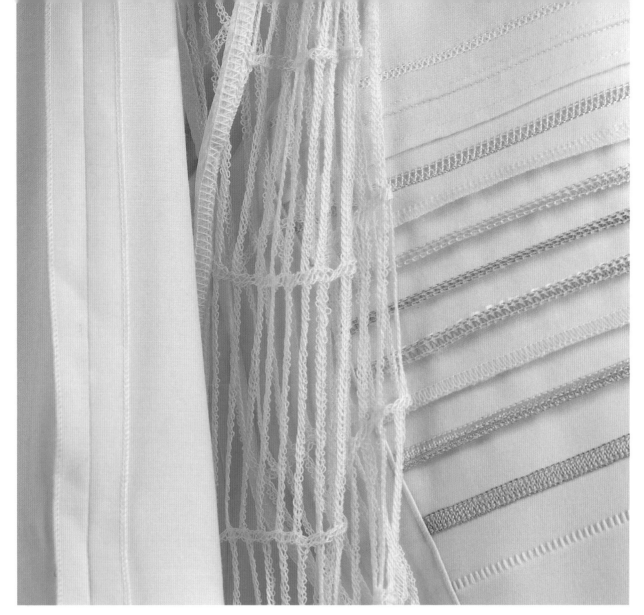

Anne's Thai Coat

I liked this pattern immediately, with the overlay springing to mind as my palette. I think Nancy thought it a little light as a winter coat, our original concept. Bear in mind that winters in Sydney are much milder (no cold white stuff!) than in Chicago, and to find fabric that would suit both our winter needs was in itself a challenge. Nancy's linen worked very well, while I found a beautifully fine Australian wool with five percent Spandex in a rich winter-white. Either coat would be perfect for autumn or spring in either hemisphere.

The overlay did indeed become my palette. I did a two-part overlay, one the floating panel of the coat, the other as an attached but floating scarf which could be worn loose, tied to the front or to the back. The rows of stitches were almost a sampler in themselves, reminding me once more of the rich effects achievable with great threads and serger simplicity.

I also added a center back seam to ensure I had as many "inside out" seams as possible, with the panel "sampler" having most stitches worked from the right and wrong sides, "upside down."

MATERIALS

Sewing Workshop Thai Coat™ pattern

Fabric following the pattern requirements, plus another length of fabric the length of the overlay.

Notions following pattern requirements.

A variety of coordinating heavy embellishment and machine embroidery threads (see below for actual thread used). Extra heavy embellishment thread of your choice will be required for the floating scarf.

Organza ribbon, 1 inch (2.5cm) wide, 4 times the length of your overlay.

Silk ribbon, ⁵/₈-inch (1cm) wide, 1 yard each in three different colors.

Water soluble stabilizer.

DIRECTIONS

NOTE: I shortened all the pattern pieces 8 inches (20cm) before I started, since the full length would have been too long for my 5 foot-3 inch (163cm) height.

- **Embellish your extra fabric with the stitches and threads listed below. Cut the coat pieces, following the pattern directions. Overlock all the garment edges except the armholes and sleeve cap.**

- **Cut the embellished overlay fabric into the two separate halves lengthwise. Cut to the fold lines of the miter on the pattern piece. Overlock the edges with a narrow 3-thread overlock when cut to size. The embellished panel will sit inside the mitered overlay.**

- **The floating scarf panel is wide coverstitch worked on water soluble stabilizer, the width and length of the inside perimeter of the floating** panel. Vertical lines were worked about 2 inches (5cm) apart. Diagonal lines hold the framework together.

- Stitch the silk ribbons across the top of the overlay with the wide coverstitch, trim ends flush with the edge of the floating scarf panel and set aside the remaining ribbon.

- When the panel is finished, cut in half lengthwise.

- Wrap the organza ribbon around the scarf edges along each side and secure with a wide coverstitch, applying liquid seam sealant to the cut ends of the organza.

- When you have completed the stitching, immerse the scarf overlay in cool water. Leave for a few minutes before swishing around in the water. Repeat as many times as necessary to remove the stabilizer. You will have loose scrappy fringed ends along the bottom edges, seal the ends with a drop of liquid seam sealant.

- Stitch a floating scarf panel into each shoulder seam.

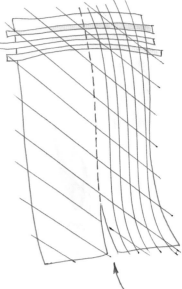

The floating scarf panel has vertical lines worked about 2 inches (5cm) apart. The diagonal lines hold the framework together. Stitch the silk ribbons across the top of the overlay. When the panel is finished, cut in half lengthwise.

- Construct the coat following the pattern instructions. With edges turned to the right side of the garment, all the mitered edges immediately are "inside out" and the hems "upside down."

- The seams that were stitched to the outside with a sewing machine straight stitch were the sleeve and center back seam. All the miters were brought to the outside of the garment. The sleeve facing was stitched to the inside and hemmed by hand.

- Tie the floating scarf overlay into an informal tassel, using some of the threads and extra silk ribbons for ties. Seal the ends with a drop of liquid seam sealant. Add silk ribbon accents to the floating scarf overlay for a little whimsy.

3-thread rolled hem with regular cone thread for most edges.

Remaining seams finished with narrow 3-thread finish with regular cone thread.

Wide coverstitch with YLI Jeans Stitch™ for floating scarf panel.

Machine straight stitch for "inside out" seam construction.

"Sampler Insert" into coat panel.

From the top row of stitching:

Narrow coverstitch from the wrong side: YLI Jeans Stitch™ in the chain looper, regular cone thread in the needles.

Narrow coverstitch from the right side: regular cone thread in the needles and chain looper.

Wide coverstitch from the right side: regular cone thread in the needles and chain looper.

Wide coverstitch from the wrong side: YLI Pearl Crown Rayon™ stitch in the chain looper, regular cone thread in the needles.

4-thread wide overlock: regular cone thread in the needles, upper and lower loopers.

4-thread wide overlock: regular cone thread in the needles and lower looper, YLI Pearl Crown Rayon™ in the upper looper.

4-thread wide overlock: regular cone thread in the needles and lower looper, YLI Pearl Crown Rayon™ in the upper looper.

4-thread narrow overlock: regular cone thread in the needles and lower looper, YLI Pearl Crown Rayon™ in the upper looper.

4-thread "decorative reinforced" overlock: regular cone thread in the needles and lower looper, YLI Pearl Crown Rayon™ in the upper looper, stitched over silk ribbon.

3-thread wide overlock: regular cone thread in the needle and lower looper, YLI Jeans Stitch™ in the upper looper.

Double edging with regular cone thread in the needles and lower looper, YLI Pearl Crown Rayon™ in the upper looper for both the passes, working

3-thread wide overlock stitch for the frist pass and 3-thread rolled hem for the second pass.

3-thread wide flatlock: regular cone thread in the needle and lower looper, YLI Pearl Crown Rayon™ in the upper looper.

3-thread wide flatlock: regular cone thread in the needle and lower looper, YLI Pearl Crown Rayon™ in the upper looper.

3-thread wide flatlock: regular cone thread in the upper and lower looper, YLI Jeans Stitch™ in the needle.

3-thread wide rolled hem with needle in the left-hand position: regular cone threads in the needle and lower looper, YLI Pearl Crown Rayon™ in the upper looper.

3-thread 2-needle stretch wrapped seam: regular cone thread in both needles and the lower looper (the upper looper is disabled with the looper) converter.

s i x

Ethereal Scarves— The Scarf Challenge

WHERE DO IDEAS COME FROM? I think as Nancy and I both ventured into our challenges, we were pushed into second guessing what the other would do. There was absolutely no difference for our Scarf Challenge. Remember, prior to the photo shoot, neither of us had seen the projects of the other nor had we discussed them (Talk about blind faith!). Our initial brief was "one long, one shawl, one other," each to have a similar color theme to our serendipitous find of the crinkled purple and lime green fabric. I think we discussed which fabric we were to use, but time has a habit of diluting the memory, even though we wrote down our concept. I will blame very sketchy notes on my part for any crazy departures from the initial brief.

I presumed that Nancy would do more structured and elegant scarves than I would. Bearing in mind our very different personalities and styles, I was not too far wrong on that count! However, her "Plaid Fiber Art" and "Ripply" scarves were terrifically artsy and sending me off to my serger post haste to reproduce.

I think Nancy felt pretty much the same when she saw my "Cobweb Shawl" and my "Artsy Craftsy Fiber Scarf." What I really believe was the best outcome for both of us as well as for you, our readers and students, is that we were both pushed to explore and experiment outside our usual comfort zone and, we hope, that will provide you with the inspiration to do the same.

You certainly don't need our permission to reinvent the rules according to your own preferences; we will encourage you to do so at every opportunity!

Anne's Scarf Challenge

I have worn scarves for as long as I can remember whether they were in or out of fashion: big, little, subtle, flamboyant, formal or feral, I have always loved the way a simple adornment can have so many interpretations. My mum (or mom for Americans) always said I could tie a shoelace around my neck and make it look good, so for me the scarf challenge was one of my most anticipated project chapters.

I decided it was time for me to go a little artsy craftsy and explore and experiment with some contemporary effects achievable only with the serger and some of the fantastic threads and stabilizers that make fantasy fabric out of otherwise conventional products. When I start exploring in this manner, I liken it to "thinking beyond the loopers."

Cobweb shawl front—Anne.

Cobweb shawl back—Anne.

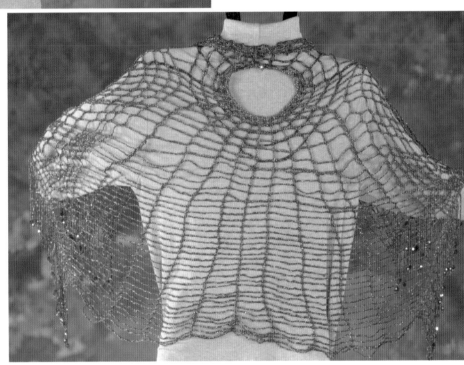

Cobweb Shawl

The cobweb shawl is made exclusively from thread and embellished with beads: it is a testimony to coverstitch and modern technology. If your serger has a large "D" zone, the shawl can be created as a single unit. If your serger has a small "D" zone, you will have to work in smaller units and join them together at your sewing machine: try some decorative embroidery stitches for real pizzazz.

MATERIALS

Glitzy thread (see below for actual threads used)

Polyester embroidery thread

Water soluble stabilizer

Beads with a moderately sized eye and beading needle

Ruler, water soluble marking pen and circle template

DIRECTIONS

- Determine the dimensions of your scarf as shown in the illustration below. Bear in mind the tape measure will not have the same flexibility as the threads.

- Cut your water soluble stabilizer to a little larger than your measurements. Trace 3 to 5 concentric rings in the center of your fabric as descibed below.

- Rule a straight line from the short end of the stabilizer until you near-

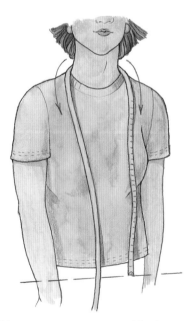

Take your tape measure and lay it around your neck to determine the length you would like your shawl to be. Determine the width of your scarf at the same time.

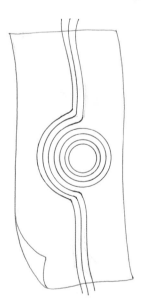

Trace 3 to 5 concentric rings in the center of your fabric slightly off center with the largest circle near but within the long edge of the stabilizer. Rule a straight line from the short end of the stabilizer until you nearly reach the outside of the circle, draw around the circle edge, and then continue with the straight line. Draw two more lines in the same manner.

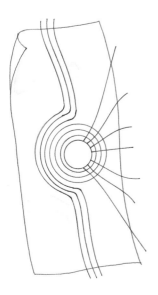

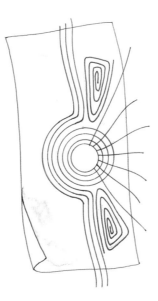

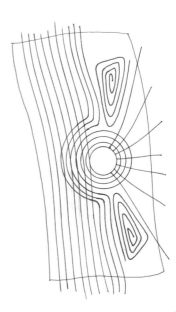

Rule spokes radiating out from the center of the inner circle along one side.

Following the diagram, fill in the angular space with a blunt-cornered concentric triangle, starting from the outside and finishing in the center of the shape.

Rule as many lines as required from one end to the other to fill in your stabilizer.

ly reach the outside of the circle, draw around the circle edge and then continue with the straight line. Draw two more lines in the same manner.

■ Rule spokes radiating out from the center of the inner circle along one side only.

■ Following the diagram, fill in the angular space with a blunt-cornered concentric triangle, starting from the outside and finishing in the center of the shape.

■ Rule as many lines as required from one end to the other to fill in your stabilizer.

■ Again following the diagram, fill in the remaining spaces with a grid.

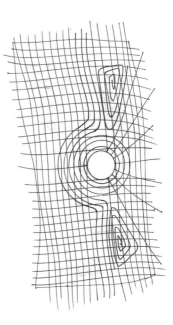

Fill in the remaining spaces with a grid.

- Stitch your shawl in the same sequence that you drew on your stabilizer.

- When you have completed the cover stitching, immerse the shawl in cool water. Leave for a few minutes before swishing around in the water. Repeat as many times as necessary to remove the stabilizer.

- Add beads to the fringed ends of the shawl and any stray ends of threads that may need them.

- This shawl design is very forgiving of any hiccups or misses that may occur: simply re-stitch or perhaps stitch a bead on by hand.

THREADS AND STITCHES

Wide coverstitch: Superior Halo™ thread in the chain looper, polyester embroidery thread in both needles.

Artsy Craftsy scarf—Anne.

Artsy Craftsy Fiber Scarf

Perhaps this should be re-titled my "idiotic adventure" scarf: I started playing with texture and kept going, not thinking too strenuously about writing instructions. With that consideration in mind, please understand that this is truly an art scarf and while I will try to make it reproducible for you, it is really about designing your own art scarf from a series of different processes and techniques.

Refer to the Cobweb Shawl for determining your scarf size and buy your fabric accordingly.

MATERIALS

Funky fabric: this could be hand-dyed silks or cottons, handwoven fabric or a terrific "mixed" fiber (aka unknown content) as our scarf fabric was.

Soft sheer fabric to contrast or harmonize with your funky fabric; this could be chiffon or georgette, natural fibers or synthetic.

Water soluble stabilizer.

Heavy cotton threads to contrast or harmonize with your funky fabric (see below for actual threads used).

Polyester embroidery threads to contrast or harmonize with your funky fabric.

Buttons, flat rings, beads or your choice of trims.

DIRECTIONS

- Starting at the center section with the sheer fabric, stitch wide coverstitch the chosen length of your scarf,: running the stitching in parallel rows for about 15 to 20 rows. Soft fabrics will ruche or pucker as you sew and may need to be held taut. Experiment a little to determine which outcome you prefer.

- Stitch about 10 to 15 rows of 3-thread overlock fabric (see Chapter 3, Serging Tapas, page 48) on each side of your gently ruched fabric.

- Cut your funky fabric in half lengthwise, overlap, and join to your 3-thread overlock fabric with one or two rows of serger chain stitch. You may choose to offset it substantially from each side of your ruched fabric as I did.

- Cut one end of the scarf at an angle and at the other end, cut away a rectangle at each corner, if not sufficiently offset.

- Fold a hem along each side of your scarf; stitch the hem in place with a narrow coverstitch.

- Make two or three serger rouleaux (see page 51) and attach to your flat rings by folding them in half, looping the folded end through the center of the ring, and drawing the ends through the folded end. Pull ends to tightem..

- Stitch roleau ends by sewing machine to your scarf.

- Optional: tie knots or stitch beads in corner of scarf.

Make 2 or 3 serger rouleaux and attach to your flat rings by folding them in half, looping the folded end through the center of the ring, and drawing the ends through the folded-end. Pull ends to tighten.

- Make a quantity of rolled hem chain and thread through your beads. Attach to your scarf with a sewing machine straight stitch. Apply liquid seam sealant to prevent any threads unraveling.

- Cut two slits into your fabric near the angled edge and work free-motion satin stitch edges around them to loop your scarf through.

- Fray some of your hems if you prefer a really de-constructed "edgy" look

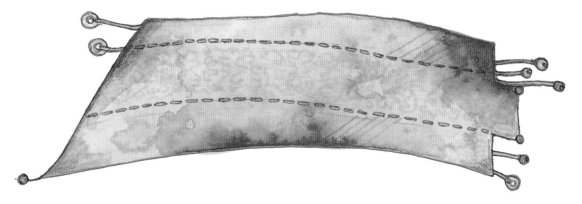

Design your art scarf from a series of different processes and techniques including, narrow coverstitch, chainstitch, 3-thread overlock fabric, coverstitch ruched fabric, beads on rolled hem chainstitch, discs on serger rouleau, and knots or beads at corners of the scarf.

Wide Coverstitch with polyester embroidery thread in the needles and Sulky 30 wt. Cotton™ in the chain looper. The stitch length was increased to 4.0.

Narrow coverstitch with polyester embroidery thread in the needles and chain looper.

3-thread overlock fabric with polyester embroidery thread in the needle, Sulky 12 wt. Cotton™ in the upper and lower looper.

3-thread rolled hem chain with polyester embroidery in the needle and lower looper, Sulky 12wt Cotton™ in the upper looper. The stitch length was increased to 2.0.

Serger chain stitch with polyester embroidery thread in the needle and Sulky 30 wt. Cotton™ in the chain looper.

Serger rouleau with 3-thread rolled hem, regular cone thread in needle and loopers.

Machine free motion zigzag stitch with polyester embroidery threads in the needle and bobbin.

Sewing machine straight stitch for applying trims.

Softly Gathered Scarf

Many of the materials used in this scarf are the same as those in the "Artsy Craftsy Fiber Scarf." A totally different, very feminine, look was achieved with very simple stitches and, once again, "thinking beyond the loopers."

Funky fabric: this could be hand-dyed silks or cottons, handwoven fabric or a terrific "mixed" fiber

Soft sheer fabric to contrast or harmonize with your funky fabric: you will need around twice the finished length to exploit the soft fabric

A variety of coordinating or contrasting heavy cotton threads and machine embroidery threads (see below for actual threads used).

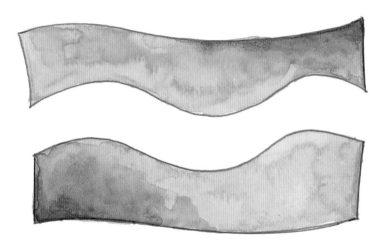

Cut your funky fabric following the general shape in the diagram.

DIRECTIONS

Funky Fabric

- Cut your funky fabric following to the diagram; that general shape is all that is required.

- Embellish the edges with a 3-thread narrow stitch with a heavy thread in the upper looper.

Soft Fabric

- Embellish the shaped edges of your soft fabric with a dense rolled hem using heavy thread in the upper looper. To gather your fabric, use a wide coverstitch with polyester embroidery thread in both needles and the chain looper; increase the stitch length to maximum and the differential feed to a greater number. Gather fairly close to the long straight edge giving you a double gather with half the effort.

- Test sew on a scrap of your fabric to determine the fullness and increase the differential feed if more fullness is preferred.

- Stretch the funky fabric into a straight line in the direction of the arrows.

- Using flower head pins, pin the fabrics in a straight line along one side. Offset the fabrics so that there are interesting lengths of layers.

- Keep the decorative heavy threads to the top.

- Stitch all layers together with 2 rows of narrow coverstitch. Add beads or tie knots in the ends of your scarf layers if preferred.

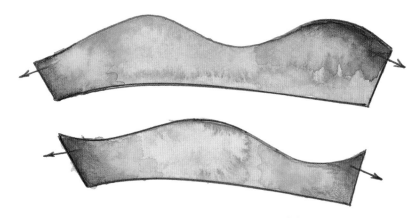

Stretch the fabric into a straight line in the direction of the arrows.

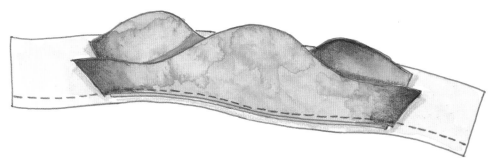

Pin and stitch the fabrics in a straight line along one side with the decorative heavy threads to the top.

3-thread narrow overlock with sulky 30 wt. cotton in the upper looper, polyester embroidery thread in the needle and lower looper. The stitch was increased to 3.0.

3-thread rolled hem with Sulky 12 wt. cotton in the upper looper, polyester embroidery thread in the needle and lower looper. The stitch was increased to the densest stitch possible without having the thread bunch up; this varies from serger to serger, so play a little to get a heavy edge.

Wide coverstitch gather with polyester embroidery thread in both needles and the chain looper; increasing the stitch length to maximum and the differential feed to a greater number.

Narrow coverstitch with polyester embroidery thread in the needles and chain looper.

Nancy's Scarf Challenge

Like Anne, I've loved scarves for as long as I can remember. Various trips abroad have reinforced the elegance that a wonderful piece of neckwear can add to the simplest outfit. I immediately fell in love with the paisley wool challis we found, was challenged by the funky mustard/violet remnant and knew in a heartbeat that my "other" project would be made up entirely of fibers. This challenge was loads of fun for me with many more ideas leaping off the springboard of Anne's pieces. We both reached beyond our limits and urge you to do the same too!

Close up detail—Nancy shawl.

Flatlocked and fringed shawl—Nancy.

Flatlocked and Fringed Wool Challis Shawl

This is probably my favorite piece in the entire book. The fabric is rich and elegantly hued with an expensive "hand". The flatlock banding technique is simple serging at its best. There is no way that you could successfully duplicate this look using a sewing machine. The addition of tiny Ultrasuede squares at each corner guarantees a professional finish to each row of flatlocking and gives a place to hide wayward stitches. I think this shawl would be the perfect gift idea for women of all ages and treasured as a valuable and versatile wardrobe element for years to come.

Fabrics:

1 $\frac{1}{2}$ yards wool challis

Small Ultrasuede scraps—enough for four $\frac{1}{2}$ inch (1cm) squares

Threads:

1 cone texturized polyester yarn—sample used **Poly Yarn by Superior Threads**

1 cone all purpose serger thread

DIRECTIONS

Cut (actually tear) as follows:

- **Pull a crosswise thread to give a guideline for tearing or cutting an on-grain fabric square. The square needs to be on grain and perfectly straight to allow for even fringing.**

- **Chalk-mark a line 2 inches (5cm) in from each of the four cut edges, marking on the right side of the fabric.**

- **Chalk-mark a dot at each corner where the lines intersect. The corner dots mark the starting and stopping points for flatlocking; do not stitch beyond the dots at the corners.**

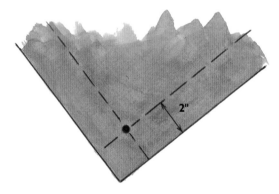

- **Set your serger for a wide, 2-thread flatlock. Place the serger thread in the needle and the texturized polyester yarn thread in the upper looper. Refer to flatlocking on page 40 in the Serger Tapas chapter for settings.**

Chalk mark lines 2 inches in from all four outer edges of the shawl. Mark the corner intersections with dots.

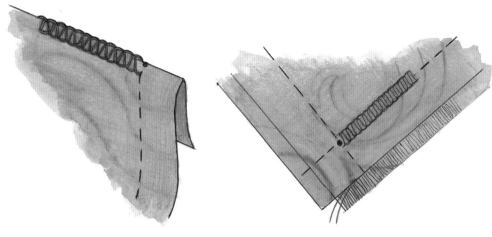

Flatlock from dot to dot on the marked line.

Pull crosswise threads below the flatlocking to create self fabric fringe.

ASSEMBLY

■ Beginning at the dot, serge in a flatlocked band along the chalked line at one edge, finishing at the dot at the opposite end of the line.

■ Repeat along the remaining edges of the shawl. Pull the flatlocking on each side of the band to flatten the stitches.

■ Weave the thread tails into the flatlocked band using a large-eye embroidery needle.

■ Using a sewing machine, sew Ultrasuede squares at the band intersections covering the start/stop points. These squares, while being decorative, can hide any irregular stitches.

■ Pull out crosswise threads below the flatlocked band creating a fringed effect. The sample shawl shows 1½-inch deep fringe.

Bias Ripply Chiffon Scarf

What do you do with exactly half of a 1⅓-yard remnant? Well, Anne and I bought before we thought and gave ourselves a challenge indeed. We both were drawn to the color and texture of this piece. Anne loved the acid green and I was taken with the violet. Out of the store we split the piece lengthwise, straight down the middle and returned to our studios to experiment. The piece was too short for my taste to stand on its own as it was. I then remembered how my serger students enjoyed roll hemming bias edges with differential feed on wovens. I hit upon the right technique. I could easily cut up my remnant on the diagonal, shuffle the pieces and serge it back together with wavy seams. Beading the side hems would add the sparkle.

- Cut chiffon yardage into diagonal strips in assorted sizes. My strips ranged from 2 inches to 4 inches wide. The remnant piece we each had was 29 inches wide x 48 inches long.

- Set your serger for a 3-thread narrow rolled hem using the directions found on page 40 in Chapter 3, Serger Tapas.

- Decrease the differential feed setting to 0.7 to make the front feed dogs move more slowly than the back and pull the fabric edges through as they are being serged. This will ripple or "lettuce" the seam.

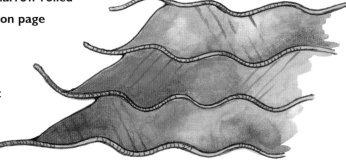

Roll hem using differential feed to create "ripply" seaming.

ASSEMBLY

- Wrong sides together, match the long diagonal edges of two strips and roll hem seam them together using differential feed. Cut to straighten up the sides and begin to form scarf rectangle.

- Continue to add additional diagonal strips until your desired scarf length is serged. Because the scarf is being created on an angle, it is important to remember to check the sides to assure that the scarf remains straight and that you are not serging a parallelogram.

- Narrow-roll hem the two long sides, leaving a 10-inch (25cm) tail of rolled hem chain for beading. Using a hand needle threader, feed the rolled hem chain through the holes in the beads. Knot each end to secure beads to scarf.

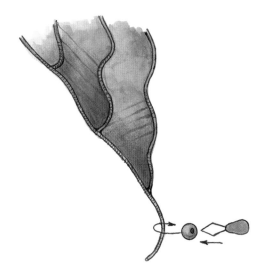

Roll hem scarf sides to straighten, leaving long hem chain tails for attaching beads.

Chainstitch Fiber Scarf

My last scarf was the one I had thought about for some time. I wanted to design a project that proved that sergers could happily sew on thin air—and this one does! Entirely created out of fun fibers and serger chain, this airy scarf was fast and easy.

MATERIALS

2 packages of AquaBond paper-backed adhesive wash-away stabilizer.

Water soluble stabilizer.

Cellophane tape.

10 packages of Designer Threads in an assortment of fibers (approximately 20 yards) for body of scarf.

DIRECTIONS

- Trim the water soluble adhesive stabilizer to the desired width of your scarf, plus $^1/_2$ inch (1cm) extra on all four sides. From the second package, cut a 12-inch (30.5cm) long piece of stabilizer the same size width as the first. Secure this add-on piece to the first with tape on the sides.

ASSEMBLY

- Follow the excellent package directions to lay out and secure the threads and fibers to the tacky stabilizer.

- When finished adding the fibers, place a single layer of water soluble stabilizer over the fibers and base.

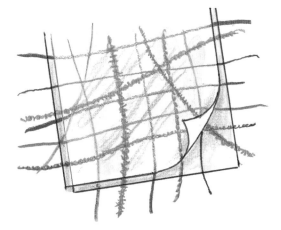

Thread fibers attached to sticky stabilizer, topped with water soluble stabilizer, ready to chainstitch.

- Set your serger for a basic chainstitch with decorative thread in the chain-stitch looper. I used two topstitch-weight threads: Oliver Twist, a hand-dyed cotton, and Mettler Cordonnet.

- Chainstitch through all layers, securing the fibers with the serger stitching. Place your rows approximately $^1/_2$ inch (1cm) apart in a grid fashion. When finishing the lengthwise rows, chain off the stabilizers, adding a row of chainstitch yardage to the fringe fibers.

- Follow the manufacturer's directions to dissolve the stabilizer away. Hang the completed scarf to dry. Carefully steam press if desired.

seven

Wardrobe Challenge

O VER THE YEARS, BOTH ANNE and I have been fascinated readers of the various sewing magazines that have run garment challenges among designers. Since we had both taught and published, we hoped that these publications would take note of our work and ask us to participate. Unfortunately, this has not yet happened, so we decided not to wait. On one of our shopping ventures at our favorite fabric store we gave ourselves the challenge for this book. Happily we browsed in the designer room of Vogue Fabrics in Evanston, IL, and quite quickly came up with a set of delicious fabrics from which to design our garments. We purchased 2-yard cuts of each of four fabrics, and $1^1/_2$ yards each of the challis to finish up that bolt.

Shown in the opening photograph is a display of the fabrics chosen, plus a wool donation from Down Under to complete our garment palette (from left to right):

Paisley 100 percent wool crepe/challis.

Violet heathered 100 percent wool flannel.

Olive green 100 percent wool basketweave.

Two toned plum strip in 100 percent wool.

Ivory tropical weight 100 percent wool batiste.

Multicolored plum tweed stripe in 100 percent wool.

We loved and admired our beautiful collection many times, blissfully unaware of the challenges that a couple of the pieces would present. Read on and follow our garment journey.

Nancy's Garment Challenge

I couldn't wait to dive into my pile of fashion fabrics. Not only did each piece "speak" to me (well, one whispered more than spoke), but I relished the thought of creating clothes for myself again. I had begun sewing when I was very young to fill my closets with lots of clothes. I loved fashion at an early age. Gangly arms and long legs necessitated learning how to sew in order to have sleeves and pant legs long enough for my growing body. Garment sewing has always held a special place in my heart. Lately, as it has for many people, life has gotten in the way of doing the things we love. This part of the challenge gave me a reason to sit down and sew beautiful clothes for myself once again. I welcomed it!

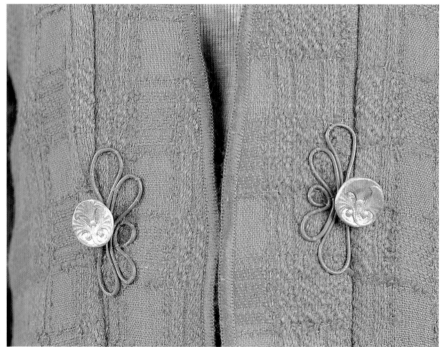

**Olive jacket Nancy—
close up detail.**

Nancy's Olive Jacket

I found this was one of my favorite pieces in the group, which was the same for Anne. The minute I saw the bolt I knew that it had to be included.

I quickly discovered, also as Anne did, the temperamental nature of the fabric due to the thick and thin weave of the patterning. But, sewing is all about creative challenges and solutions. I think the finished garment works well and shows that we can tame any yard goods put in front of us.

I wanted a simple jacket pattern to allow the fabric to showcase. Loes Hinse's "Bolero Jacket #5106" was perfect. As I read the pattern I discovered that the primary directions call for its being put together on a serger. What a perfect choice!

DIRECTIONS

- Cut the jacket following the pattern directions.

- Thread your serger for a 5-thread seaming using a chainstitch and overlock combination. This is the suggested construction stitch mentioned in the pattern. Use all-purpose serger thread in all positions.

ASSEMBLY

- Serge-seam the jacket following the very clear pattern directions. The only assembly change that I made was eliminating the seam attaching the front and back neck facings to the outer jacket edge. Because I knew that I was going to finish this edge with an overlock stitch, I simply placed the facing and jacket edges wrong sides together and basted them close to the cut edge.

- Press the jacket. Anne and I both discovered that we needed to have a careful hand in pressing this loosely woven wool.

WOOLEN SERGED EDGE FINISH

I think what makes this jacket subtly elegant is the beautifully coordinated wool edging. As I've said many times before, use simple techniques and beautiful fabrics and threads for spectacular results. This edge finish elegantly illustrates the point.

- Set your serger for a wide (left needle) 3-thread balanced tension overlock seam. Place all purpose serger thread in the needle and wooly decorative threads in both the upper and lower loopers. Monet thread by YLI is a perfect choice for a non-shiny, subdued, and slightly fuzzy edge. Decrease your stitch length to 2.0 or lower so that the stitches touch closely.

The 5-thread chainstitch and overlock serger seaming combination are perfect for loosely woven wools.

- Serge along the entire outer edge. Fold up the sleeve hems and repeat the serger edge finish.

- I fashioned frog-like accents at the button placement using 2mm-wide olive green leather cording, hand-sewing it in place. Attaching handmade raku ceramic buttons completed this understated and beautiful garment.

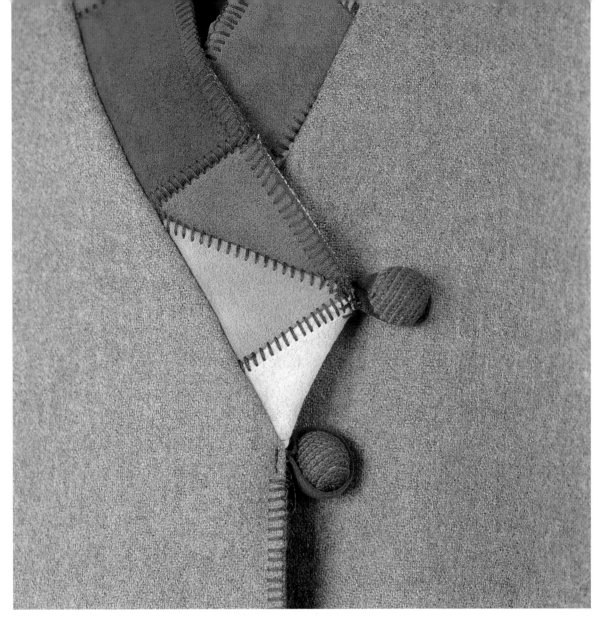

Heather vest detail—Nancy.

Nancy's Flatlocked Ultrasuede Vest

Loving to be able to create effects not found on the sewing machine is one of my favorite serger exercises. I wanted a vest that would showcase flatlocking in its finest application. Purrfection Artistic Wearables Kimono Jacket and Vest pattern #1007 gave me the ideal simple collar design to carry a flatlock pieced band. Over the years I've accumulated a respectable sized stash of Ultrasuede scraps. Digging in the box produced several complimentary pieces to coordinate with the heathered wool.

MATERIALS

Purrfection Artistic Wearable Kimona Jacket and Vest pattern # 1007.

Woolen fabric, yardage as indicated on pattern.

Lining fabric.

Ultrasuede scraps in coordinating colors.

Threads (see directions for actual threads used).

Fusible interfacing for collar.

Wash-away stabilizer.

Unfinished wooden beads for buttons.

Tacky glue.

DIRECTIONS

Cut vest and lining following the pattern directions. Cut only one collar piece since the second will be comprised of the Ultrasuede scrapwork.

CREATING THE COLLAR BAND

- **Fuse interfacing to the wool collar. Fold the ⁵⁄₈ inch (1.5cm) seam allowance towards the interfacing side of the collar, along the outer edge. Set aside.**

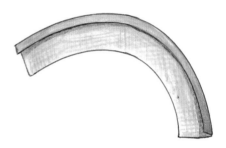

Interfaced collar band with seam allowance pressed towards the interfacing.

- **Set your serger for a wide, 2-thread flatlock. Follow directions for flatlocking set up on page 40 in Chapter 3, Serger Tapas. Install a size 90 topstitch needle into the left needle position. Thread this needle with topstitch-weight thread. I used Cordonnet by Mettler. Thread the lower looper with all-purpose serger thread.**

Cut random scraps of Ultrasuede large enough for the width of the collar.

- **To flatlock-piece the suede scraps together, place two pieces right sides together.**

Ultrasuede pieces right sides together, flatlocked.

Serge seam together. Pull the seam flat on the left and right edges of the seam. The serged stitches will flatten beautifully and the distinctive "ladders" will show at the seamline.

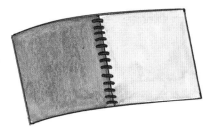

- Repeat the flatlocking process until a collar-sized piece is assembled.

- Carefully pin the suede collar piece to the wool collar piece along the pressed edge of the wool.

"Ladders out" stitches showing after the flatlock seam is pulled flat side to side.

BLANKET STITCHED COLLAR EDGE

The outer edge of the collar is finished with a 2-thread blanket stitch using wash-away stabilizer as a pulling aid to straighten out the needle stitches. Refer to page 43 in Chapter 3, Serger Tapas, for serger set up.

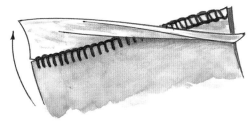

- Using the blanket stitch directions, serge the suede and wool collar pieces together along the collar's outer edges.

Water soluble stabilizer on top of the right side of a finished edge, ready to serge in blanket stitch flatlock. Water soluble stabilizer pulled to left after flatlocking to straighten needle stitches into a blanket stitch formation.

- Pull the serged stitches straight, using the stabilizer to manipulate.

- After the needle part of the blanket stitch is pulled flat, carefully remove
  the stabilizer by hand. Use a pair of sharp-tipped embroidery scissors and tweezers to remove the excess from within the underside of the stitching.

- Sew the complete collar unit to the vest following the pattern directions.

- Complete assembling the vest following the guidesheet.

- Accent the outer and armhole edges of the vest with serger blanket stitches to continue the garment design.

ROLLED HEM BUTTONS

Not finding just the right buttons for this vest, I used my serger to create custom cord-covered buttons with a filled rolled hem and wooden beads. The resulting buttons blend beautifully since they are made up of threads used in the vest itself.

DIRECTIONS

- **Set your serger for a narrow 3-thread rolled hem.**

- **Install a cording accessory foot onto the serger. It will hold multiple filler cords so that a more rounded hem chain can be stitched.**

- **Cut two or three strands of topstitch-weight thread and place them into the cording foot.**

- **Thread your serger for a rolled hem with all-purpose serger thread in all positions.**

- **Serge yards of rolled hem chain over the filler cord.**

- **Glue the completed filler cord over _unvarnished_ wooden beads. Begin by securing the thread tail near the hole in the bead using a tacky glue. Allow the thread tail to dry so that it does not move as you encircle and glue additional rows.**

- **Add successive rows, completely covering the bead. Glue and clip the tail at the opposite hole in the bead. Hand-sew onto the vest through the hole.**

- **Use leftover Ultrasuede strips to fashion the button loops. Machine-sew in place.**

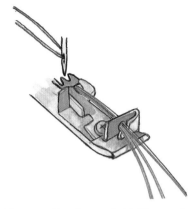

Use a cording foot to hold filler cords while serging for a more rounded and thicker rolled hem chain.

Glue and wrap the rolled hem chain to a drilled wooden ball for a unique button closure.

Plum fabrics—collection of garments.

Plum Stripe Skirt

I love the vertical lines of this skirt which gives the wearer extra height and makes you look pounds lighter! I wanted a simple skirt with an elegant serger touch that was a discreet serger accent. A single wrapped edge on the overlap found in a McCall's skirt pattern fit the bill.

Stripe skirt detail—Nancy.

MATERIALS

Commercial wrap skirt pattern of your choice.

Woolen tweed fabric, yardage as indicated on pattern.

Topstitch-weight thread and all-purpose serger thread.

Any additional items as indicated on your pattern.

DIRECTIONS

■ Cut skirt following the pattern directions.

■ Set serger for a 2-thread wrapped edge found on page 43 in Chapter 3, Serger Tapas. Thread the needle with all-purpose serger thread and topstitch-weight thread in the lower looper.

■ Construct the skirt fronts, creating the overlap.

■ Serge in a wrapped edge on the side front foldline. The wrapped edge will appear as a custom binding on the fabric.

■ Complete the skirt following the guidesheet.

■ This skirt is easy and elegant, and uniquely customized by using your serger talents!

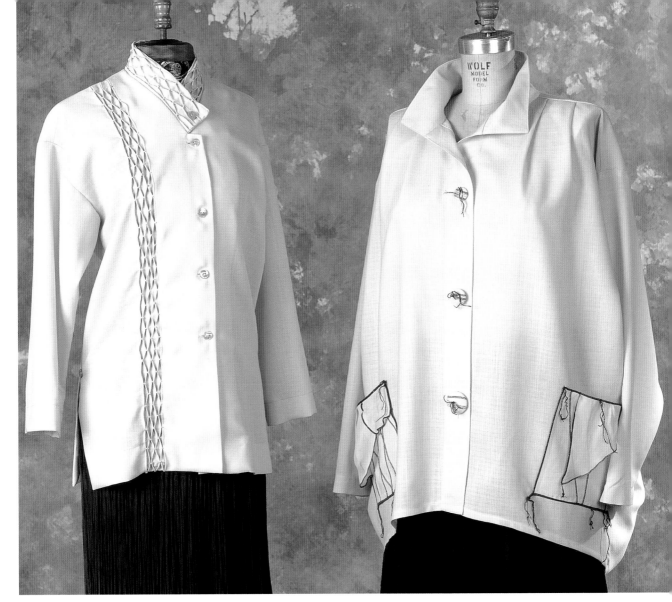

Beaded Basketweave Big Shirt

Anne had come through with her promise to find some beautiful Aussie fabric to add to our garment collection. When she showed me the yardage all I could think of was that it was the worst possible color for me to wear. It was great for Anne with her healthy coloring, but I am much paler and need color near my face. However, the hand of the fabric was exquisite, soft, and drapable. I decided that this was what creative sewing was all about and set to design something that was elegant and simple. The Basketweave Shirt was born. I think I surprised Anne too, since she was going to serge one for herself.

MATERIALS

Shirt pattern: Elle Shirt and Pant by The Sewing Workshop.

Subtly variegated embroidery thread: Variations by YLI, and all-purpose serger thread.

3mm pearl beads.

Beading or very fine handsewing needle.

DIRECTIONS

- For one blouse front and the upper collar piece, cut large rectangles of fabric 6 inches wider than that needed for the pattern piece. This extra width allows for excess used by the tucks.

- Cut the remaining blouse pattern pieces following the guidesheet.

ROLLED HEM TUCKS

- Center the pattern piece for the uncut blouse front on the extra width of fabric. Determine the approximate positioning for the tucks on the fabric. Draw a line or crease mark this position with an iron.

- Set your serger for a 3-thread narrow rolled hem. Place the variegated thread in the upper looper and all purpose serger thread in the needle and lower looper.

- Fold the fabric wrong sides together along the marked line. Serge in the first rolled hem tuck.

- Using your presser foot as a guide, refold the fabric and serge tucks 2 and 3 a presser foot width away from the previous tick.

- Reposition your fabric and fold, then serge three more tucks an equal distance away from the first tuck going in the opposite direction. You should have a total of six tucks.

- Carefully steam press the tucks to smooth.

Basketweave beading technique—in progress.

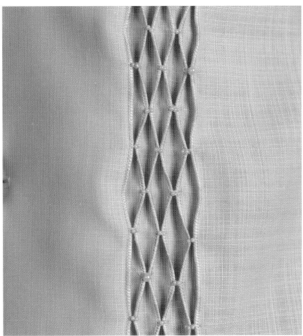

Basketweave beading technique—finished, Nancy.

BASKETWEAVE BEADING

- Pinch a pair of tucks together and, using a handsewing or beading needle, tack a pearl at the point where the two tucks touch. Working in a straight line across, pinch each pair of tucks and tack a pearl where they touch.

- Working in rows evenly spaced ³/₄ inch (2cm) apart, alternate the bead placement on adjacent tucks on each row across to create a Basketweave, or diamond, pattern.

- Bead both one shirt front and the upper collar rectangles.

- Carefully cut out pattern pieces from the embellished yardage.

- Construct the shirt following the pattern directions using a balanced tension, 4-thread overlock.

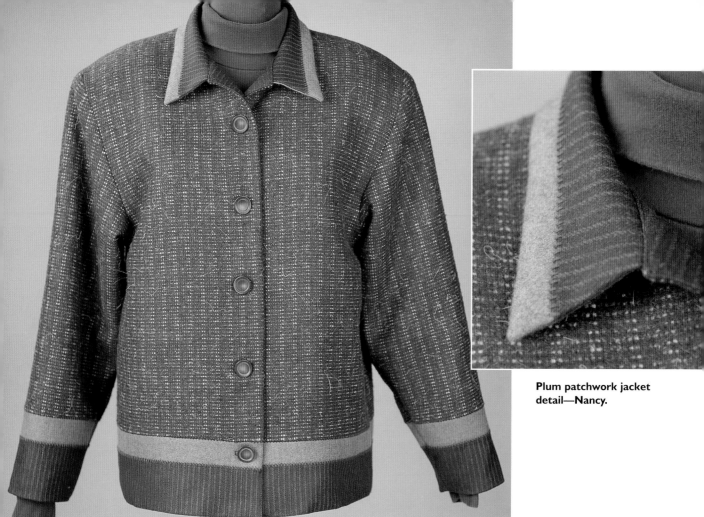

Plum patchwork jacket detail—Nancy.

Plum patchwork jacket—Nancy.

Plum Jacket Collage

This last garment was my nemesis. I had started a first jacket using a different pattern with unusual design elements from a favorite pattern manufacturer. Somewhere between the written pattern directions and my serger were many crossed signals. As Anne was soon to arrive, I had a completely unusable jacket and only scraps leftover from my original 2-yard piece. Anne had already finished her collection and panic set in, the same as she told me she had with her olive jacket. But I didn't have the luxury of sending an S.O.S. to Anne for her leftovers because she was in the air. Long story made short, we proceeded with the photo shoot without my jacket, Anne sent me her scraps and I cobbled together this lovely jacket. I just love it. The "Easy Street Jacket" by Four Corners was a blissfully simple and pleasurable jacket to finish off my challenge easily.

MATERIALS

Jacket pattern.

Lining fabric.

Woolen fabric and added fabric for banding.

Topstitch-weight thread and all-purpose serger thread.

DIRECTIONS

- Cut the bulk of the jacket pieces, approximately 75 percent of length, from the main fabric, allowing for about 4$\frac{1}{2}$ inches (11.5cm) of added fabric at the lower edge.

- Cut bands of heather and stripe flannel wide enough to achieve the full length pattern pieces needed.

NOTE: Flatlocked strips of fabric were both the fabric stretching and design elements in this jacket. Approximately 4$\frac{1}{2}$ inches of bands were needed to stretch the main jacket fabric to the needed length. I carried through the flatlock design elements onto the jacket collar to unify the garment.

FLATLOCKING TO STRETCH YOUR YARDAGE

- Set your serger for a wide, 2-thread flatlock. Use a size 90 topstitch needle threaded with topstitch-weight thread. Place all-purpose serger thread in the lower looper.

- Right sides together, flatlock the fabric bands together. Pull the stitches flat and steam press to set. Flatlock the two-pieced band to the jacket body.

- Repeat the same process on the collar using a 1$\frac{1}{2}$-inch (4cm) band flatlocked to the lower edge of the collar.

- Construct the jacket following the pattern directions.

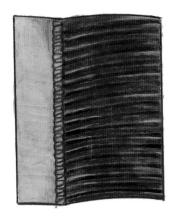

Use "ladders out" flatlocking to collage fabrics together to extend yardages.

Anne's Wardrobe Challenge

The wardrobe challenges presented our very first challenge at the fabric store: our different hair color, body shape, and style preference. I have coppery red hair, albeit chemically enhanced now, while Nancy is very dark with a different red highlight. While I have always tended to be more "out there" in my garment style, Nancy has always had a more classic wardrobe.

We found the fabrics, a happy and comfortable agreement between us. We could use the fabrics with whichever pattern we preferred and did not discuss in any way what combinations of fabric and patterns each of us was to use. The patterns were a bit trickier because Nancy physically required less fabric for her garments. Though she is taller than I am by a long way, I am wider than she is by a long way. We elected to use commercially available patterns as well as those from independent pattern designers. See how we handled these "no rules" challenges very differently.

Olive jacket Anne—close up detail.

Green Wool Jacket

MATERIALS

Kwik Sew™ pattern # 3129, view A.

Woolen fabric, yardage as indicated on pattern.

Small amount of striped wool for lapels.

Buttons in 3 different sizes.

Threads (see below for actual threads used).

DIRECTIONS

- I cut the facings from the self striped wool which can also be seen as lapels depending upon how the jacket is being worn. I serged all the edges first and then joined all the fabric sections with a regular sewing machine stitch.

- I immediately decided to use the triple coverstitch and contrasting needle threads along what were the machine topstitching lines in the pattern guidelines, as well as across the stripe in the top of the lapels, chain piecing all the sections together with no practice piece first . . . can you see where this is heading?

- I was totally unprepared for the resulting finish: because of the nature of the weave, the fabric did not sit as smoothly as I thought it would and it looked uneven. Being way past the point of no return because undoing the stitching would have damaged the fabric, I had to work out how to fix my problem. A sense of panic had set in because being an ocean away from the fabric store in Chicago, I knew I could not chance being able to get more yardage. I turned my sewing room upside down looking for a rayon knitting thread I knew I had somewhere and finally found it. I couched it along the seamlines with a zigzag stitch at the sewing machine and with great relief, found that it worked out well.

- I chose to use three different-sized buttons, graduating from small to large for added interest to the jacket.

- On reflection, I would recommend what we are always told and what we recommend to our students: Sew a sample first, especially on unusual fabrics. I would have no hesitation making up the same pattern again with a different fabric.

STITCHES AND THREADS

Triple Cover Stitch with YLI Colours™ for jacket body, collar and lapel detail.

3-thread wide overedge with regular cone thread for seam neatening.

Sewing machine straight stitching with regular polyester thread for construction.

Sewing machine zigzag with YLI Colours™ for applying cord.

Self-Striped Wool Jacket

This was more of an "ask" for me, since this was probably my least preferred fabric color. I used the Loes Hinse Bolero jacket in the shorter length because I had already used some fabric to cut the lapels for the green wool jacket. Good planning yet again!

MATERIALS

Loes Hinse Bolero Jacket pattern #5106.

Striped woolen fabric.

Threads (see below for actual threads used).

Flat knitting ribbon.

DIRECTIONS

- I used heavy thread in a coordinating color to the wool, with needle threads matching the fabric. Using a narrow 3-thread stitch and stitch length of 3.5, I chained off about 20 yards (20 meters) of fine cord, encasing a variegated flat knitting ribbon at the same time. At the sewing machine, I stitched half the cords to my jacket lapels in gentle curves with the ribbon side uppermost, using the machine braiding foot and a straight stitch. The jacket ties were made with multiple cord lengths which were hand-twisted using the serger spool pin as an anchor, to create a textured Monk's cord (see below).

STITCHES AND THREADS

- **3-thread narrow overedge with regular cone thread for seam neatening.**

- **3-thread narrow overedge with YLI Pearl Crown Rayon™ in the upper looper, polyester embroidery threads in the needle and lower looper encasing variegated flat knitting ribbon for cords.**

- **Sewing machine straight stitching for construction.**

- **Sewing machine straight stitch with braiding foot for applying cord.**

Making Monk's Cord

- **Take eight 2-yard (2-meter) lengths of the cords plus four lengths of the flat knitting ribbon and fold in half creating a looped end.**

- **Tie a knot in the loose ends of the threads.**

- **Secure the other end to the vertical spool pin of your sewing machine or serger.**

- **Insert a pencil in the inner loop.**

- **Hold firmly and keep the threads taut at all times.**

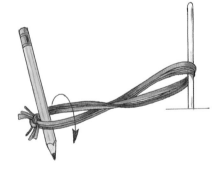

Tie a knot in the loose ends of the threads. Secure the other end to the vertical spool pin of your sewing machine or serger. Insert a pencil in the inner loop.

- Use the pencil to twist the threads in one direction only.

- When the threads start to kink on themselves, take hold of the threads at the center.

- Take both ends towards one another, holding taut at all times.

- Release the twists from the centre of the threads about 4 inches (10cm) at a time.

- Smooth or ease any kinks out as you go, as the threads form a twisted cord.

- Tie both knotted ends together securely, attach to jacket seams following the pattern instructions.

Smooth or ease any kinks out as you go, as the threads form a twisted cord.

Patchwork jacket—Anne.

Collaged Woolen Jacket

The Dragonfly™ pattern by Diane Ericson gave me enough flexibility to combine fabrics in a jacket that reflects my personal style well. It also reflects that I had side-tracked myself with another project before I did this one and subsequently did not have enough of any one fabric to make a skirt or pants to follow the original concept we had hatched, hence the collage of fabrics.

MATERIALS

Dragonfly™ pattern by Diane Ericson.

Assorted fabric pieces.

Silk fabric to make ribbon strips and lining

Threads (see below for actual threads used).

Fusible fabric.

Spray starch.

Rotary cutter, ruler, and mat.

DIRECTIONS

- **Rotary cut a variety of squares and rectangles from your fabric selection, laying them out on fusible interfacing which is slightly larger that the actual pattern piece. Leave a ¹/₄ inch (6mm) gap between the fabrics both horizontally and vertically, varying the placement of the horizontal rows on each half of the jacket. Fuse when you are happy with the layout.**

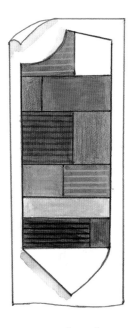

Rotary cut a variety of squares and rectangles of your fabric selection, laying them out on fusible interfacing which is slightly larger that the actual pattern piece.

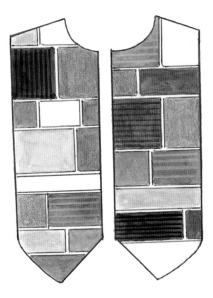

Leave a ¹/₄-inch (6mm) gap between the fabrics both horizontally and vertically, varying the placement of the horizontal rows on each half of the jacket.

- Make 5 yards (5 meters) of 1-inch (2.5cm)-wide ribbon with one of the optional fabrics. I used a subtle silk with a hand-dyed look with a double-edge stitched down each side of silk strips to create the ribbons. Use the ribbon to make the vertical lines with irregular intervals, keeping the horizontal lines more regular..

- Apply the vertical ribbon strips to the fabric first with a wide coverstitch, each length cut immediately prior to being applied.

- Once all the vertical strips were applied, the horizontal ribbons were applied and then the garment was finished following the pattern instructions. The hems were stitched with 2 parallel rows of wide coverstitch.

- The remaining silk fabric for the lining was stabilized with spray starch and then enriched with very simple sinuous lines of narrow coverstitch.

STITCHES AND THREADS:

- Double edging with **YLI Colors** in the upper looper, polyester embroidery threads in needle and lower looper along the edge of 1-inch (2.5cm) silk strips.

- Narrow coverstitch with **Superior Halo** for silk lining.

- 4-thread overlock with regular cone thread for construction.

- Wide coverstitch with polyester embroidery threads in the needles and **YLI Monet**™ in the chain looper.

- Sewing machine straight stitching.

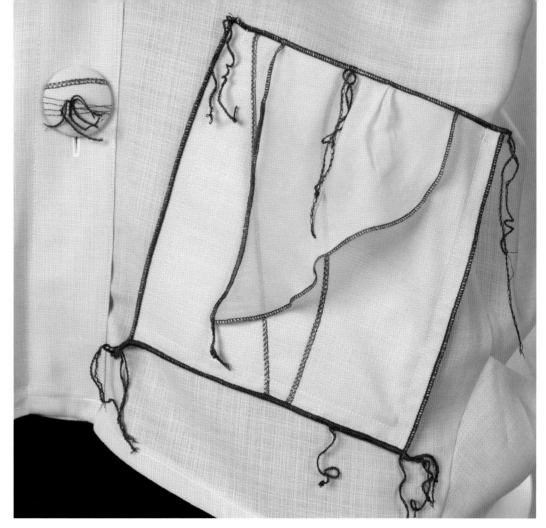

Ivory blouse—Anne.

Big Shirt

PAW Prints™ "The Big Shirt" was my first choice for this summer-weight wool, for a casual overshirt or as a jacket with a sleeveless shell. The pattern was made following the directions and only the pockets and buttons were embellished.

MATERIALS

PAW Prints™ "The Big Shirt" pattern.

Fabric, yardage as given on pattern.

¼ yard (20cm) silk chiffon.

Threads (see below for actual threads used).

Liquid seam sealant.

Self-cover button kits in three sizes.

DIRECTIONS

■ For the pockets, work on an interfaced piece of fabric larger than the finished size. Serge rows of 3-thread rolled hem at an angle and then add narrow coverstitch.

■ From the piece of silk chiffon, cut simple triangles from each short side of the chiffon and edge each side with a regular 3-thread rolled hem, going over the same stitching twice, catching the second row of stitching into the top of the pocket and the other edges remaining loose. Leave all the thread chains intact as you serge off the ends of the fabric, then secure them with a small dot of liquid seam sealant. In addition make about 2 yards (2 meters) of rolled hem chain for the shirt buttons, leaving the serger settings at the manufacturer's recommendation. Stitch the pockets to the jacket by sewing machine.

■ As for the green wool jacket, I chose to use three different sized buttons, graduating from small to large: Use self-covered button kits and embellish a length of fabric with simple narrow cover stitch, worked from both sides of the fabric. Trap short lengths of thread chains in the stitching for a 3-D effect and then make the buttons following the directions on the packet.

STITCHES AND THREADS

3-thread rolled hem with Superior Halo™ in the upper looper for pocket and button trim.

3-thread rolled hem chain with regular cone thread for extra button trim.

3-thread narrow stitch with regular cone thread for garment neatening.

Narrow coverstitch with Superior Halo™ in the chain looper and regular cone thread in the loopers.

Sewing machine straight stitching for construction.

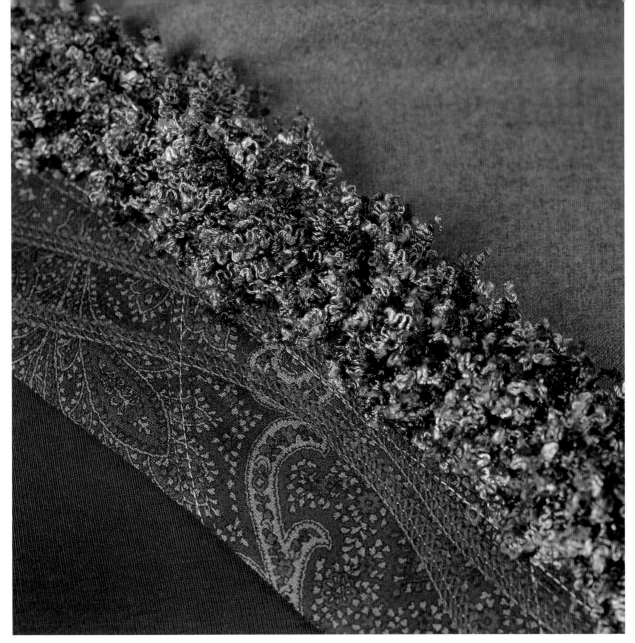

Woolen Shawl

This was supposed to be either pants or a skirt, but in my haste to cut everything else out first, I did not have enough of any fabric to make a "bottom." No worries, to improvise with another garment was my immediate reaction!

I chose the heather wool which I still had a full length of, plus the paisley wool to edge the shawl. I also included a funky furnishing trim which Nancy and I had bought on a previous fabric shopping expedition.

MATERIALS

2 yards (2 meters) heather flannel.

Paisley challis for trim.

Threads (see below for actual threads used).

DIRECTIONS

■ **Neaten edges of the 2-yard length of fabric by trimming off the selvages. Hem the cut edges with the wide coverstitch.**

■ **Cut one piece of the paisley fabric, the width of the shawl from side to side (plus seam allowances) and 8 to 10 inches (15 to 20cm) in length. Interface this piece and triple coverstitch at random over the fabric from both sides. Fold the paisley fabric in half in the direction of the scarf width, right sides together, and stitch down each of the short side. Turn to the right side. The finishing trim was then applied across the fabric.**

■ **Stitch one side of the paisley trim pocket to the shawl edge, with the right sides of both the paisley and the shawl together: Turn the paisley border over the edge of the shawl to encase the edge. Turn under the raw edge of the paisley trim and sew by machine to the shawl.**

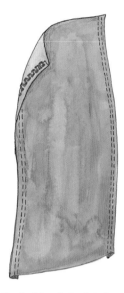

Each side of the fabric length was first neatened and the wide coverstitch used as a hem down both sides.

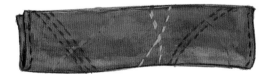

The paisley fabric was interfaced and triple coverstitch stitched at random over the fabric from both sides.

The shawl body was stitched along one side of the paisley fabric only, with the fabric and shawl body right sides together.

- 3-thread narrow stitch with regular cone thread for garment neatening.

- Wide coverstitch with polyester embroidery threads in the needles and YLI Monet™ in the chain looper.

- Triple coverstitch with polyester embroidery threads in the needles and YLI Monet™ in the chain looper.

- At the sewing machine, straight stitch to apply furnishing trim.

- Hand stitching to finish wrong side of paisley application.

eight

Home Decorating Challenge

Anne's Home Decorating Challenge

This was my most challenging theme: I think Home Wreck rather than Home decorating is more what I thought before I began. Nancy and I selected fabrics while I was in the US and determined our challenge criteria: we were both to make a pillow (yes, we call them cushions in Australia), a table topper, a tieback for me specifically and then our individual choices of project if we had sufficient fabric left over. When I suggested something "touchy feely" for part of the theme I am not really sure what Nancy thought I was up to. While I have certainly made my share of pillows, I have generally used patchwork fabrics and embellished them as class projects or gifts. As for making a curtain tieback, that doesn't even come anywhere near my radar because we don't have or need curtains at home with views out to the bush. My feeling was Yuk (and then double Yuk), so this was a real mountain for me to get over. I kept it as simple as I possibly could and, yes, Nancy you can have the left-over fabric for your house since it matches perfectly!

Fabric for challenge.

FABRICS USED IN HOME DECORATING CHALLENGE
(from left to right)

Gold Rayon and Cotton Jacquard.

Sage Green Floral Cotton Jacquard.

Gold Box Dotted Cotton and Rayon.

Burgundy and Gold Striped Cotton Sateen.

NOTE: Small amounts of a variety of other fabrics from our personal collections were also included in our home decorating projects.

Tactile Toys

These geometric shapes just scream out to be touched, held and admired. While not really designed for children to play with, who is not going to argue that they meet all the criteria of soft toys for adults as well?

MATERIALS

Fabric to be cut into rectangles twice as long as they are wide. Anne used 6 x 3 inches (15 x 7.5cm), 5 x 2½ inches (12.5 x 6.25cm) and 4 x 2 inches (10 x 5cm).

Very firm interfacing cut to the same size as fabric rectangles, less ¼ inch (6mm) seam allowances.

Thread (see below for actual threads used).

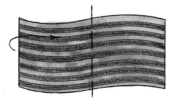

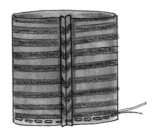

Stitch the short edges of a fabric rectangle together with a _-inch (6mm) seam allowance.

Refold fabric so the seam is now at the center front. Stitch across the bottom edge of the fabric.

Stitch in from each end of the remaining open seam, leaving an opening.

Turn to the right side through the opening. Fill with craft batting and slip stitch to finish.

DIRECTIONS

- Fuse the interfacing pieces to the wrong side of the fabric rectangles.

- Chain stitch the short edges of the fabric together with a $^{1}/_{4}$-inch (6mm) seam allowance.

- Refold fabric so the seam is now at the center front.

- Straight stitch across the bottom edge of the fabric.

- Refold bag with the first row of stitching to the side; hold the first row of stitching at the open end, matching raw edges and creating a pouch.

- Stitch in from each end of the remaining open seam, leaving an opening.

- Turn to the right side through the opening.

- Fill with craft batting and slip stitch finished.

STITCHES AND THREADS

Chain stitch with polyester embroidery thread in the needle and chain looper YLI Pearl Crown Rayon™ in the chain looper.

Curved table topper—Anne.

Curved Table Topper

Simple chainstitch and gently curving design lines coupled well with our home decorator fabric selection and rich embellishment threads. Playing with curves, solids and stripes, Anne re-engineered the look of the striped fabric: it appears quite different depending upon the angle it is viewed from.

MATERIALS

$1/2$ yard (45cm) striped decorator fabric.

$1/4$ yard (22.5cm) each of two solid decorator fabrics.

Backing fabric

Piping cord and piping foot

Lightweight fusible batting

Rotary cutter, mat, and ruler

Heavy decorative threads, polyester embroidery thread

DIRECTIONS

- **Overlap the ends of the fabrics with the right side of fabric facing up. Using a rotary cutter and mat, cut a gentle curve.**

- **Repeat for as many segments you want and until you get the length you require. With right sides together, seam adjoining pieces at the sewing machine with a straight stitch.**

- **Press to one side, clipping curves as required to ensure fabric lies flat.**

- **Work parallel rows of chainstitch from the wrong side of all the fabrics once they are joined in gentle curves, keeping the numbers of rows uneven for best visual effect.**

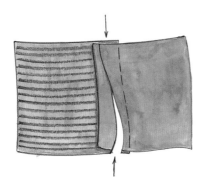

Place both fabrics right side up on cutting mat, overlapping slightly. Cut a gentle curve using a rotary cutter. Repeat for the number of pieces you require for your table topper.

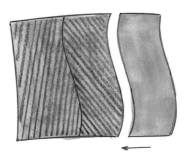

Join each piece at the sewing machine with a straight stitch. Press to one side, clipping curves as required to ensure fabric lies flat.

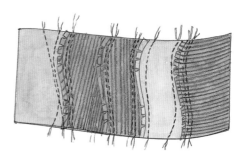

From the wrong side, work parallel rows of stitching on each side of the seamlines. For best visual effect, work odd numbers of rows.

- Cut striped fabric on the bias into strips wide enough to wrap around cord and allow 1 inch (2.5cm) for seams. Join strips at a 45-degree angle. Wrap, wrong sides together, around cord to make the piping. Again using the piping foot, stitch the piping to the circumference of the runner.

- Fuse lightweight batting to the wrong side of the embellished topper.

- Place the backing fabric on top of the topper, right sides together. Using the piping foot once more stitch around runner leaving a 4-inch (10cm) opening left to turn the topper through. Once turned through, slipstitch the topper closed.

STITCHES AND THREADS

- Chain stitch with polyester embroidery thread in the needle **YLI Pearl Crown Rayon**™ in the chain looper.

- 4-thread overlock stitch and piping foot to make and apply piping.

- Machine straight stitch for joining segments.

- Slip stitching by hand to finish topper.

Pillow with Ruched Binding

MATERIALS

$^1/_2$ yard (50cm) of decorating fabric with narrow regular stripe.

$^1/_2$ yard of contrasting decorating fabric (at least 54 inches wide) for piping.

$^1/_2$ yard of coordinating decorating fabric for pillow back.

2 strips contrasting fabric twice the length of the piping cord: measure loosely around

7 feet ($2^1/_4$ meters) thick piping cord for ruched edging.

Heavy decorative threads, polyester embroidery threads.

Chalk marker and ruler.

Tearaway stabilizer.

Flower head pins.

Lightweight fusible batting.

Pillow form.

3 buttons for back closing.

DIRECTIONS

Note: Fabric amounts generally are enough to make two 20-inch (50cm) pillows, but more striped fabric is required to allow for embellishment and extra piping cord is also required.

Preparation

- **Cut the fabrics as follows: For the striped fabric, cut one 2-inch (5cm) strip along the long edge for flat piping; cut in half across for 2 lengths. Cross-cut the remaining fabric into three 8-inch (20cm) strips (Called fabrics #1, #2, and #3 below).**

- **Cut the contrasting piping fabric into enough 4-inch (10cm) wide stripes to measure 14 feet long when joined (twice the length of the piping cord).**

- **From the coordinating fabric, cross-cut two pillow back pieces, each 12 x 20 inches (20 x 50cm).**

- **Embellish your striped fabric (see below for suggested embellishment), working from the wrong side with heavy decorative thread in the chain stitch looper and polyester embroidery thread in the needle. The decorative stitches form on the right side of your fabric. Test-stitch first to see which results you prefer.**

- **Striped Fabric #1: Stitch every few rows along the stripe on either the light or dark bands. Each method yields a different effect.**

- **Striped Fabric # 2: Stitch with the stripe at wider intervals. Rule chalk lines across the strips to form rectangles and stitch along these lines.**

- **Striped Fabric #3:** Stitch across the stripes at narrow intervals, butting the presser foot up to the previous row of stitches, using the presser foot as a guide for width.

- Select the striped fabric you prefer as your center front fabric, trimming it to measure 7$\frac{1}{2}$ x 21 inches (20 x 55cm). Cut the two remaining embellished fabrics to the same measurement, one for each side of the pillow.

- Embellish the 2-inch (5cm) wide flat piping strips as follows: Working across the strips and starting 4 inches (10cm) in from one end, stitch three lines of chainstitch, with the two outer lines spaced 2 inches (5cm) apart and the third line between in a contrasting color to give a ribbon-like appearance. Stitch two or three embellished bands across each strip. Note: Because the fabric is narrow, it is easier to start and finish stitching onto a length of stabilizer for each row.

Ruched Piping

- Join the 4-inch (10cm) wide cut strips along the short ends at a 45-degree angle, right sides together. Wrap the fabric strip over the cords, wrong sides together. Stitch the fabric and cord together at one end to anchor the cord with a long stitch for the first 4 inches (10cm); continue stitching the length of the fabric, pushing the excess fabric back along the cord, distributing the fabric evenly along the length of the cord. Starting at the open end of the piping, and midway along one side of the pillow, pin with flower pins to the pillow front, matching raw edges. Pin all around the pillow front; when you are back to the beginning, tuck in the ends of the piping so they will be encased by the seam when the back of the pillow is attached. Stitch the piping in place, using a zipper foot to get as close to the piping as possible.

Pillow Backing

- Fuse a strip of interfacing to the wrong side of the pillow backs at the center edge to be turned under. Press under the edge of each back and make three evenly spaced buttonholes along the folded edge of one back.

■ Fuse batting to the wrong side of the pillow front; trim off excess batting so edges are even. Matching raw edges, place the buttonholed back over the front, with right sides together. With the right side facing down, place the remaining back piece over the uncovered half of the front, matching raw edges and having the center edge overlap the buttonholed back. Serge around all edges with a balanced 4-thread stitch using your piping foot. Then stitch in place at the sewing machine using a zipper foot so that you can get as close as possible to the piping. Secure each corner with seam sealant, trimming thread chains when thoroughly dry. Turn the pillow cover to the right side. Sew on buttons to back opposite buttonholes. Insert pillow and button closing.

Curtain Tieback

Make the tieback to your desired length after taking accurate measurements. It is made with the same embellished fabrics from the pillow with ruched binding. If you are making just the tieback, refer to the pillow instructions for embellishment detail.

MATERIALS

Printed decorator fabric.

Backing fabric.

6 inches (15cm) decorator fabric to contrast with the print.

Contrasting fabric for piping.

Scraps of embellished fabric from the pillow with ruched binding.

Backing fabric.

Piping cord and piping foot.

Lightweight fusible batting.

Rotary cutter, mat, and ruler.

Heavy decorative threads, polyester embroidery thread.

Buttons, needle, and handsewing thread.

METHOD

- Fuse batting to wrong side of print fabric.

- To make three tube strips of embellished fabric scrap from your pillow, cut three strips of fabric 2 x 6 inches (5 x 15cm). With right sides together, sew along the long side; turn right side out.

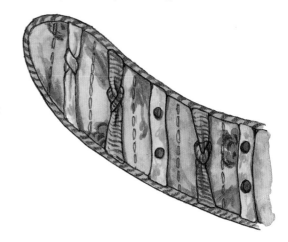

- To make four tube strips from your pillow scraps, cut four strips of contrast fabric 2 x 6 inches (5 x 15cm). Sew with right sides together, and turn right side out. Tie a knot in as many strips as you wish.

- With flower head pins, pin all strips at an angle on the tieback.

Pin all strips at an angle on the tieback.

PIPING

- Cut bias strips of a second contrast fabric; join narrow ends to form long strip. Wrap fabric over cord, wrong sides together. Stitch fabric and cord together at one end to anchor the cord with a long stitch for the first 4 inches (10cm). Using piping foot, stitch length of wrapped strip to make piping

- Apply piping with the piping foot to the right side of the tieback. Place the front and backs on top of each other, right sides together. Serge around all edges with a balanced 4-thread stitch, using your piping foot or your sewing machine with a zipper foot, leaving an opening. Turn through to the right side and slip stitch open edge.

- Stitch buttons to your unknotted strips.

Nancy's Home Decorating Challenge

I *love* to sew home decorating! Beginning when my children were small until about a year ago I used to work with a variety of private clients and decorators to create unique window treatments, pillows, table toppers and just about anything fabric oriented to put into a room. I love the weight and textures found in decorating goods, so much different from quilting or garment fabrics. My own 1920s home is highly stylized. From painted ceilings to faux finished walls, my vintage house is antique-filled with inherited family pieces and purchased ones. Living with turn-of-the-century Victorian furniture naturally leads my decorative tastes towards luxurious fabrics in rich colors. Do I love tassels and trims? Of course! I look for visual richness in my personal decorating and always urge my students to push themselves one step further to add just a tiny bit more when working on a project to add richness to theirs. As Anne and I were brainstorming the book, the inclusion of home decorating projects was a given for me. I felt totally at ease as we shopped decorator fabric stores for our challenge pieces. Serge home decorating? Bring it on!

Square in a Square table topper—Nancy.

Square in a Square Table Topper

What a lovely way to enjoy beautiful fabrics and add a jewel-like accent to a plain table. This topper looks a lot harder than it really is. Featuring mitered corners and a beautiful satin stitched band, you'll be surprised to find that it can be put together in a couple of hours. The best part of this project is that after it was finished, I found a similar design in a French import store. It was slightly smaller, had no button accents but a whopping $145 price tag. Grinning from ear to ear, I exited the store knowing how happy it would make all you serger readers. Isn't this part of why we sew?

MATERIALS (for a 39" square topper)

Fabrics

Two coordinating home decorating pieces, one a 54-inch (137cm) square for the back and front hem bands, the other a 25-inch (63cm) square for the center.

8" fabric square of solid lightweight fabric for covered buttons.

Two cones heavy decorative thread.

I cone all-purpose serger thread.

Assorted embroidery-weight rayon threads.

Temporary fabric adhesive spray.

Four 1½-inch (4cm) size buttons to cover.

DIRECTIONS

■ Trim the selvages from both squares assuring that the trimmed pieces remain perfectly square.

■ Thread the serger for a wide, balanced 3-thread over-lock stitch. Place the heavy decorative threads (I used Pearl Crown Rayon by YLI) in both loopers and serger thread in the left needle. Decrease stitch length to 2.0 or lower so that the serged stitches touch closely to resemble a continuous ribbon appearing band.

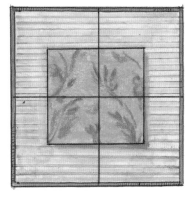

■ Serge all four outer edges of the large square. Press the overlocked edges flat.

Center and position the right side of the smaller square on top of the wrong side of the larger square.

■ Quarter-fold both the large and small squares.

■ Lay the large square, right side down, on a flat surface.

■ Lightly spray the wrong side of the smaller center square with fabric adhesive spray.

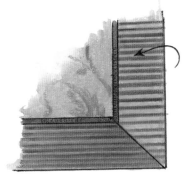

■ Center and place the smaller square right side up, using the quarter-fold lines to help match centers and keep the inner square straight. Smooth the square in place.

■ Fold up 7½-inches (19cm) of the large square fabric to make a 7-inch (18cm) hem with the cut edge overlapping the center square by approximately ½ inch (1cm). Press. Repeat on the remaining three sides.

Fold up the serge finished hem allowance on the larger square to meet and slightly cover the lower edge of the smaller square. Miter corners and stitch in place.

Creating the Corner Miter

- **Open out one pressed corner. Fold up the corner at a 45-degree angle, with the corner fold touching the corner of the pressed melines. Pin and press in the angle fold.**

- **Open up the pressed angle and trim the excess away from the lower edge, leaving approximately a ¹/₂-inch (1cm) allowance below the fold. Repeat on the three remaining corners.**

- **Fold up hems and pin all mitered corners and hems in place.**

- **Pin the serged edge of the hem allowance over the center square unit.**

- **Using a sewing machine, stitch the serged edge of the hem in place, securing it to the center square.**

Button Accents

- **Texturize plain fabric with decorative threads that coordinate with the decorator fabrics for unique corner accents.**

- **Chainstitch irregular rows onto plain fabric. Use this "sergerized" fabric to cover 4 large buttons. Sew in place at the corner junctions.**

Serger Smocked Pillow

Differential feed, a feature unique to our sergers, allows us to create row upon row of delicate smocking in a heartbeat to add a subtle and tactile touch to a simple accent pillow.

MATERIALS: (for a 10 inch x 14 inch pillow)

Fabric

Lightweight fabric for smocked center, 8 inches wide x 42 inches long
(sample used silk dupioni; fabric *must* be lightweight to serger-smock).

For sides, back, and piping, approximately ¹/₂ yard of 54-inch (137cm)-wide
fabric.

Threads (see directions below for suggestion).

Pillow form.

Notions

1¹/₃ yard (1¹/₄ meters) brush fringe.

²/₃ yard (61cm) of ³/₈-inch (1cm) wide piping filler cord.

10 inch x 14 inch (25cm x 35cm) pillow insert.

Cut a center panel 8 inches (20cm) wide x 42 inches (107cm) long from the lightweight fabric.

From other fabric cut two front sides 7 inches (18cm) wide x 14 inches (35.5cm) long, a back 17 inches (43cm) wide x 14 inches (35.5cm) long, two bias piping strips each 2 inches (5cm) wide x 14 inches (35.5cm) long.

DIRECTIONS

- Set your serger for "Stable Chainstitch Smocking" found on page 42 in Chapter 3, Serger Tapas. Use a rayon thread in the chainstitch looper for an elegant and decorative effect.

- Using a fabric-marking tool, draw a lengthwise center line vertically on the wrong side of the center panel fabric.

- Chainstitch smock (see Chainstitch Smocking, page 42 in Chapter 3, Serger Tapas) on the drawn line. Serger smock successive rows approximately ¹/₂ inch (1cm) apart. You need not draw additional lines if you use the width of your serger presser foot as a guide for spacing rows.

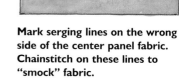

Mark serging lines on the wrong side of the center panel fabric. Chainstitch on these lines to "smock" fabric.

- Lightly steam the serged yardage to even out smocking and set the gathers.

- Trim the center panel to 6¹/₂ inches (16.5cm) wide x 14 inches (35.5cm) long.

- Create piping from the bias-cut fabric strips using the serger piping directions found on page 47 in Chapter 3, Serger Tapas.

- **Attach the finished piping pieces to the right and left vertical edges of the smocked center panel. Use a balanced 4-thread overlock stitch and a special piping foot made to accommodate the bump of your filler cord.**

- **Serge seam the side panels to the smocked and piped center.**

- **Serge seam the back to the front, leaving an opening for turning and pillow insertion. Turn right side out.**

- **Insert the pillow form, slipstitch the opening closed.**

- **Cut the brush fringe in half. Using a sewing machine, sew the trim to both the front and back side edges of the pillow for a lush, full look. Compress the pillow form at the sides to allow the trim to be sewn on with the pillow already stuffed.**

Serger Tassel—Nancy, Tieback—Anne.

"Over the Top" Serger Tassel

There isn't any room in the house that wouldn't look lovelier with the addition of a tassel of some sort. Over the years I've collected many sizes and shapes of tassels and wanted to create something for the book that was unique. I didn't want a shy tassel either. Looking at the challenge fabrics I realized that I had not yet used the green floral jacquard. I had purchased a very large wooden tassel head and didn't relish the idea of chaining off miles and miles of serger yardage to create a long enough tassel skirt. Narrow, wire edged fabric strips became a fast and easy substitute that would balance out the weight of the top of the tassel. The wire edges also allow you to mold the loops to have as wide or narrow a tassel as you would like. What great fun!

MATERIALS

Fabric

Two rectangles, each 10-inch (25cm) x 14-inch (35.5cm) coordinating home decorating fabrics.

Ruffle, 1-inch (2.5cm) x 24-inch (61cm) strip lightweight fabric.

Notions

Large wooden tassel head (sample is $5^{1}/_{4}$ inches (13cm) tall x 4 inches (10cm) wide.

Gold spray paint.

Decorative threads for custom cording.

Two 3 yard lengths of 2mm-wide firm filler cord (sample used roman shade pull cord).

Fusible web spray in a can.

26-gauge craft wire (found in beading section of most craft stores).

Wire cutter.

Hot glue gun and glue sticks.

Tacky glue.

12-inch beaded fringe, enough to encircle the bottom of the tassel head plus $^{1}/_{2}$ inch overlap.

DIRECTIONS—TASSEL SKIRT

- Spray the wooden tassel head with gold paint. Set aside to dry.

- Following manufacturer's directions, lightly spray the wrong side of one of the fabrics chosen for the tassel skirt loops with fusible web. Fuse to the wrong side of the coordinating fabric. Cut the fused rectangle into eight 1-inch (2.5cm) wide strips. (Note: Eight strips were needed to encircle the bottom of my tassel head. You may need to adjust more or less depending upon the form you are using.)

- Cut two wires for each strip, making them the same length as the strip. "Wire hem" each long strip on both long edges.

Use a serger cording foot to guide the wire while roll hem finishing tassel skirt strips.

Use a rolled hem setting and the 26g wire inserted into a serger cording foot designed to hold the wire in place while you stitch.

■ Fold the wired strips in half to create loops. Glue the loops to the bottom of the tassel form using a hot glue gun.

■ Glue the beaded trim over the loops covering the top raw edges.

GATHERED RUFF

■ Roll hem both long edges of the 1-inch x 24-inch ruffle strip.

■ Set your serger for a chainstitch, increasing the differential feed to 2.0 to serge gathers. Chainstitch along the center of the hemmed strip.

■ Hot glue the gathered strip to the bottom of the tassel head, covering the header of the beaded trim.

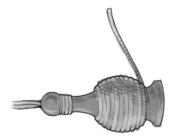

Wrap and glue the tassel head with cord filled rolled hem cording.

SERGER CORDING ACCENT

■ The top of the tassel is decorated with a custom cording that is simple and an enjoyable way to work with your newest decorative threads.

■ Set serger for a narrow rolled hem with a decorative thread in the upper looper position. I used Variations™ thread by YLI.

■ Using a cording foot attachment threaded with the 2mm firm filler cord, roll-hem over the cord, encasing it in a decorative thread chain tunnel. Serge as much yardage as you would like to cover approximately a third of the top of the tassel head.

■ Use additional cord and a spinning tool, such as The Spinster, to create the hang cord from leftover custom cording. Insert into the hole at the top of the tassel head, glue it in place, and enjoy!

■ **Serge additional wire fabric strips and add multiple layers to the tassel skirt.**

■ **Add a layer of longer beads underneath the wired loops for sparkle and movement.**

■ **Double the layer of ruffles topping the fabric strips.**

■ **Alternate the fabric choices used in the skirt loops for visual interest. Consider a satin loop next to an organza one, velvet next to brocade, and on and on . . . the possibilities are endless!**

nine

Quilt Challenge

ANNE AND I BOTH FELT that it was important to show quilters that our beloved sergers could live in their world, too. From simple, extra strong serger seaming, to quilt-as-you-go techniques, we both strongly urge our quilting friends to take a new look at how their projects are assembled. We also wanted to explore art quilts created with the serger. Rather, I should say *Anne* wanted to explore art quilts more than I. Anne falls into art projects easily and effortlessly with fabulous results. I have a more studied approach to creativity. Begrudgingly I agreed to try to stretch my talents. I had bulldozed Anne into home decorating, and isn't turnabout fair play? In the end, we both were very pleased with our results. The projects are true to our individual serger personalities and very do-able for all skill levels of serger fans. Read on and enjoy our lap quilt and "art" pieces.

Pieced Quilt front—Nancy.

Pieced Quilt back—Nancy.

Nancy's Quilt Challenge—
Reversible French Provençal Lap Quilt

I wanted to serge a simple beginner's quilt with tremendous visual impact. For years I've been teaching my students to master a simple technique then make your project sample exceptional by using fabulous fabric. This quilt certainly fits the bill. This simple quilt as-you-go project looks terrific thanks to the strong, graphic nature of the striped yard goods. It is truly a beginner's project that looks anything but.

The quilt is begun in the center and grows towards the outer edges by the addition of fabric and batting strips. Bands of fabric and batting are seamed all at once to create self-quilted and enclosed seams. Similar to a sewing machine technique, serging this process produces a flatter and more discreet fabric/batting seam than that sewn with a sewing machine. The looper threads condense all layers into a smooth, very flat seam allowance.

This quilt can be made as small or as large as you would like just by working the desired number of strips. Directions are given for a lap-sized quilt.

MATERIALS (FOR A 45-INCH X 56-INCH LAP QUILT)

Note: Double all yardages to make this quilt reversible. This is also a great project for using up fabric leftovers.

Fabric

Center panel, 12½ inches x 16½ inches (32cm x 42cm)

Strips, 2 yards (2 meters) total for each side.

Cotton batting: purchase a full-sized quilt batt to allow adequately for strip cutting.

Notions

Four cones serger thread for piecing.

Two cones heavy decorative thread for outer serger braided edge.

Temporary fabric adhesive spray.

Cut two fabric and one batting 12½ inches x 16½ inches (32cm x 42cm) cotton batting

Strips will be cut approximately 4 to 5 inches (10 to 13cm) wide depending on the prints that are chosen. I chose a multi-colored stripe that allowed

me to economize on the number of fabrics I bought. I let the printed stripe dictate the cut size of each row added to the quilt.

Set serger for a balanced tension, 4-thread basic overlock stitch with all-purpose serger thread in both needles and both loopers.

DIRECTIONS

The easiest way to understand this technique is to think of it as serging together quilt sandwiches, three layers with fabric, batting, and fabric.

Center

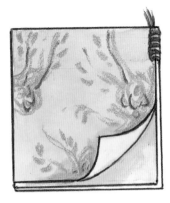

Center beginning quilt "sandwich."

- Lightly spray one side of the cotton batting with the fabric adhesive spray. Center and adhere the first center panel to the batting. Repeat spraying the remaining surface of the cotton batting, adhering the reverse side center panel.

- Serge all 3 layers together on all 4 sides.

Adding the Top and Bottom Strips

- Right sides together, place 1 front fabric strip on the right side of the top of the front center panel. Repeat, placing the right side of the back fabric strip on right side of the same top edge of the back center panel. Pin both strips in place.

Adding fabric and batting strip sets to the center quilt sandwich to build quilt.

- Pin a same-sized piece of cotton batting on top of the back top fabric strip.

Your *six*-piece quilt sandwich should be:

- Front top fabric strip, right side down

- Front center panel, right side up

- Quilt batting for center panel

- Back center panel, right side down

- Back top fabric strip, right side up

- **Strip-sized piece of quilt batting**

- **Serge seam through all six layers. Your serger will handle all this bulk effortlessly, condensing the seam into a flat, smooth line.**

- **Repeat the layering and seaming process on the opposite lower edge of the center panel. Press the seams flat.**

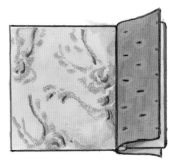

Flip the serged strips to encase the seam.

- **Turn out the serged on fabric and batting strips away from the center panel. You will see that the seam will be entirely enclosed and quilted. Isn't that great?**

- **Pin the unsewn edges of the strips. Trim the sides even with the center panel.**

- **Continue to build your quilt by adding strip sets to the side edges.**

- **When you have added strips completely around the center, press well and square up your quilt top.**

- **Add additional strips in the same order: at top and bottom and then at side edges until you have built the quilt to the size you desire.**

EDGE FINISHING

Bound Edges

Traditional quilt binding can be applied using a serger. Use your favorite binding size and substitute a 4-thread serged seam in place of a sewing machine stitched one. You can even sew in the mitered edges as you are used to. The advantage of a serged tunnel of fabric is that is will give extra support to the binding wrapping around the quilt's edge.

Serged Braid Edging

My favorite way to finish a quilt-as-you-go quilt is to use a simple, wide overlock and beautiful threads to compliment the fabrics I have chosen. The Provençal quilt is finished with two colors of Pearl Crown Rayon by YLI to tie together the reversible color theme.

- **Thread your serger for a wide, 3-thread balanced overlock stitch. Place regular serger thread in the needle and the decorative threads** in the upper and lower loopers. Decrease your stitch length to 2.0 or lower to serge so that the stitches touch closely.

- Edgestitch the outer edges of your quilt together on a sewing machine using monofilament thread in the needle.

- Carefully place the basted edge of your quilt into the serger and over-lock the edge. The bulky threads will serge a braid-like trim that is a rich finish to your project.

- Unravel and weave thread tails into the serged edge and the quilt itself to finish the corners.

Nancy's "Art" Quilt—"Ode to O'Keefe"

This was the toughie for me. To be honest, I tried to beg off this project with Anne, only to be reminded that someone had to serge home decoration, which was definitely not her cuppa tea. I agreed to stretch creatively, but put this project off until the absolute last moment.

I thought and thought, shuffled through serger technique scraps until I came upon a discarded technique scrap that was not used in this book. I had used the chainstitch to "texturize" some organza with thoughts of using it in my linen Thai coat. It didn't make the creative cut while the project was being serged, but the sample was too interesting to throw away. Looking at it reminded me of the delicately rippled veining found on the petals of a poppy which is one of my favorite flowers. I realized that I could cut gently curving petals from this texturized fabric, wire-hem the edges and turn them into flowers. I could work with everything I enjoy: simple but stunning serger techniques, beautiful fabrics, quilting, embroidery, and honoring one of my favorite artists, Georgia O'Keefe. By George, I've got it!

MATERIALS

Flowers

1/3 **yard (30cm)** *each* **silk organza in red, wine, orange, and yellow.**

8-inch square scrap black silk or polyester organza for flower center.

Background

1/2 **yard (50cm) cream silk dupioni.**

2/3 **yard (60cm) green silk dupioni.**

Leaves

1/4 **yard (20cm)** *each* **green silk organza and green satin.**

24-inch (61cm) square cotton batting.

NOTIONS

Assorted decorative threads in various fibers for veining. Sample uses 30 and 40 wt. rayon, variegated hand-dyed cottons, metallics.

26g craft wire in red, orange, and gold (wire found in the beading section of most craft stores).

Wire cutters.

Assorted black beads.

Water soluble stabilizer.

Fabric adhesive spray.

Liquid fabric sealant.

Embroidery Design. Sample uses Oklahoma Embroidery Supply and Design (OESD) design FL #794—poppy and leaves.

Hoop for embroidery.

- Select one piece of silk organza for petals.

- Cut two pieces of water soluble stabilizer the same size as the organza. Spray the stabilizer with fabric adhesive spray and adhere to both the top and bottom of the organza piece.

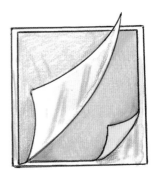

Single layer of silk organza centered between a top and bottom layer of water soluble stabilizer.

- Set your serger for decorative chainstitching. Refer to page 41 in Chapter 3, Serger Tapas, for settings. Place the decorative thread in the chainstitch looper position and all-purpose serger thread in the needle.

- Chainstitch through all layers of the stabilizer and organza fabric sandwich. Create wavy lines and change the chainstitch thread often for visual interest.

- Repeat the chainstitch texturizing process for all the fabrics chosen for the petals.

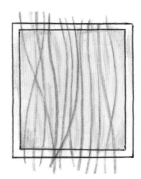

Chainstitch through all layers with multiple rows of decorative thread chainstitching.

- Remove the stabilizer by soaking the chainstitched fabric and stabilizer in a basin of warm water. Several rinsings may be needed to remove all of the stabilizer. Blot the excess moisture and allow to dry. Note: the silk fibers in the organza will crinkle as they are drying. This is the perfect effect for our petals!

- Using the petal pattern, cut out a total of 10 petals for each poppy. Do not worry if you need to piece petals. The natural linear patterning of the stitching will hide a rolled hem seam if needed.

Poppy petal pattern piece.

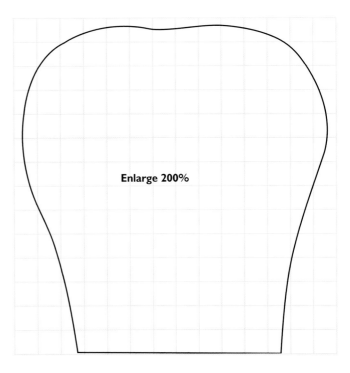

Enlarge 200%

- Set your serger for a narrow rolled hem. Install a cording or accessory serger foot designed to hold wire and filler cords. Cut a length of color-coordinated 26g wire and feed it through the foot.

- Wire-hem the outer edges of each petal allowing it to crinkle as it is being hemmed.

- Lightly hand-gather the straight base of each petal. Pull the stitches slightly to create soft gathers at the end of each petal. Set the wired and gathered petals aside.

Poppy petal cut from chainstitch embellished, washed silk and wire-hemmed.

QUILTED BACKGROUND

- From cream dupioni, cut one $14^{1}/_{2}$-inch (37cm) square.

- From green dupioni, cut one 3-inch x $14^{1}/_{2}$-inch (7.5 x 37cm) wide strip for top sashing, $4^{1}/_{2}$-inch x $14^{1}/_{2}$-inch (11.5 x 37cm) wide strip for bottom sashing, 3-inch x $19^{1}/_{2}$-inch (7.5 x 49.5cm) wide strip for left side sashing, and $4^{1}/_{2}$-inch x $19^{1}/_{2}$-inch (11.5 x 49.5cm) strip for right side sashing.

- For batting and backing, cut a 22-inch square each from cotton batting and green silk.

ASSEMBLY

- With sewing machine, sew sashing to each edge of the cream center in this order: top, bottom, left side, and right side, making $5/_{8}$-inch (1.5cm) seams.

- Press all seam allowances towards the dark side.

- Lightly spray the cotton batting with fabric adhesive spray. Center and place the pieced top onto the batting. Repeat spraying on the back of the batting to attach the backing fabric.

- At the sewing machine, free motion quilt through all layers as desired to secure them together.

- Bind the outer edges of the quilt using your favorite binding method.

- Determine the poppy petal placement. Arrange the petals in two circles, 5 petals each, overlapping the petal edges. Leave about a 1½-inch (3.5cm) circular opening in the center for the poppy center to sit. Hand-stitch the base poppy petals to the quilted background.

- Cut two 2-inch (5cm) circles of lightweight cardboard. Cover them with same-sized circles of cotton batting. Cut slightly larger circles out of black organza. Sew random small black beads to the organza to simulate the seeds at the poppy center.

- Run a basting thread around the perimeter of the beaded organza circle. Insert the batting and cardboard circle. Pull the basting threads tight to encircle and cover the fillers.

- Set your serger for a narrow rolled hem with a topstitch-weight thread in the upper looper. I used Mettler Cordonnet cotton thread in the sample. Chain off approximately 5 yards of black rolled hem yardage.

- Cut the rolled hem yardage into 2-inch (5cm) long pieces. Attach a small bead at one end of the piece by knotting above and below the bead to secure it onto the chain. Glue or hand-stitch the unbeaded end of the 2-inch chain to the wrong side of the covered circle. Note: I used approximately 40 hem chain pieces per poppy center, distributing them evenly around the circle.

- Position and slipstitch the beaded and fringed poppy center to the middle of each flower, with the beads showing around the edge of the circle.

- Crunch and mold the finished flowers, arranging them to look as lifelike as possible.

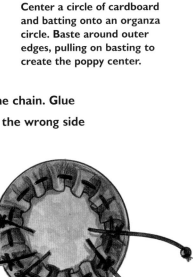

organza

fleece

cardboard

Center a circle of cardboard and batting onto an organza circle. Baste around outer edges, pulling on basting to create the poppy center.

Roll hem stamens are attached to the wrong side of the fabric enclosed cardboard circle before sewing onto the center of the poppies.

VINES

- Using your fabric scraps, cut 1¼-inch (3cm) wide bias tubes.

- Follow the directions on page 51 in Chapter 3, Serger Tapas, to create serger rouleau strips. Hand-tack rouleau strips down onto the green sashing.

EMBROIDERED LEAVES

Organza leaves

- Adhere a top and bottom layer of water soluble stabilizer to the green organza.

- Insert the stabilizer and fabric sandwich into the hoop and embroider. Note: I chose not to stitch out the full leaf embroidery because I wanted to have the fabric show inside the leaves. I stitched out only the veining and outlines.

Poppy center and veining detail— Nancy.

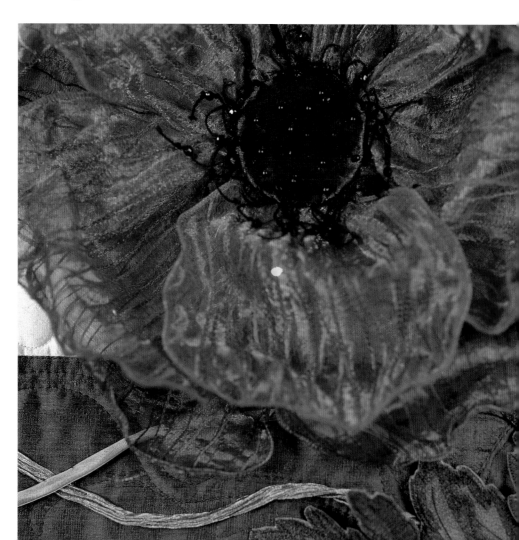

- **Remove as much top stabilizer by hand as possible. The bottom stabilizer remains within the leaves to stiffen the form.**

Satin leaves

- **Adhere only a bottom layer of water soluble stabilizer to the green satin.**

- **Insert the stabilizer and satin sandwich into the hoop and embroider the design.**

- **Remove the stabilizer from the outer edge of the satin leaf, leaving the rest inside the design.**

Trimming Both Types of Leaves

- **Coat the outer leaf edges with a liquid fabric sealant, such as Fray Chek or Fray Stoppa. When the sealant is bone dry, carefully trim away the excess from the outer edges.**

- **Position and hand-tack the leaves where desired on the wall hanging. I enjoyed placing them outside the sashing for added interest.**

- **Create and sew on a hanging sleeve and quilt label to identify your serger art piece for generations to come!**

ABC quilt—Anne.

Anne's ABC Crib Quilt

My final design and method for the quilt challenge, the ABC crib quilt, is different from my initial concept. For some reason I decided not to do "quilt as you go" at the serger, rather choosing a more traditional piecing method, which was just as well since Nancy chose to do the "quilt-as-you-go" serger technique . . . trans-Pacific ESP?

I kept to the fabric color selection very easily, immediately choosing strong colors of gold, red and green quilting cottons with both contrasting and blending threads. I elected to enrich each fabric with decorative stitching and then design a very simple quilt which could be pieced either at the serger or at the sewing machine. I kept it very modular in concept; in fact the entire pieced center of the quilt is based on a 6-inch (15cm) finished unit, lending itself to conventional piecing or using the "quilt as you go" technique. Whichever method you choose, it's as easy as ABC.

Finished Size: Approximately 45 x 60 inches (115 x 150cm).

MATERIALS

$1/2$ **yard (50cm) of red cotton fabric.**

$1/2$ **yard (50cm) of gold cotton fabric.**

$1/2$ **yard (50cm) of green cotton fabric.**

$1/4$ **yard (25cm) of medium bright blue cotton fabric.**

$5/8$ **yard (60cm) of dark blue cotton fabric for flange and binding.**

$2/3$ **yard (70cm) of striped fabric for outer border.**

Backing fabric.

Batting.

Threads for serging (see "Stitches and Threads" below for actual threads used).

Thread and needle for tying.

Thread and needle for hand finishing binding.

ABC . . . 123 embroidery disc.

- Cut the selvage from all the fabrics prior to embellishment or specific cutting.

Red fabric

- Work 3-thread narrow, 3-thread rolled hem and 3-thread wide stitches in rows across the fabric width at random intervals, working one stitch at a time. **Do not overfill the fabric with stitches or the seams may not lie flat when you piece your quilt.**

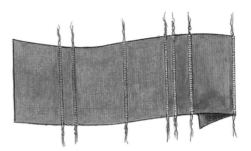

3-thread narrow, 3-thread rolled hem and 3-thread wide stitches are worked across the fabric at random intervals.

- Work rows of triple, wide and narrow coverstitch perpendicular to the previous 3-thread embellishments, using variegated threads in the needles. **Ensure the embellished rows all lie in the same direction as you stitch over them.**

From the right side of the fabric, work rows of triple, wide and narrow coverstitch perpendicular to the previous 3-thread embellishments.

Gold Fabric

- Work wide and narrow coverstitch in large gentle curves across the fabric from either the top or the bottom of the fabric at random. Repeat the same curved nature of stitching with chainstitch, from the top and bottom of the fabric.

Wide and narrow coverstitch and chainstitch worked in large gentle curves across the fabric at random.

Green Fabric

- Work wide coverstitch in meandering, but not overlapping curves, with the needle tension loosened about 1 whole number, so that the needle threads show as a defined part of the stitching. **Increase the stitch length to the maximum. In the chainstitch looper, alternate** heavy thread with neon thread which "zings" the green fabric. Lower the foot pressure so that the fabric can be turned in tight curves and diminishing circles. Cover the entire piece if fabric.

NOTE: If your serger has a large "D section," you can work the stitching on your uncut green fabric. If your serger has a small "D section," you will have to work in smaller modules and ensure that you have a little more fabric to allow for neatening, straightening and perhaps joining your modules.

Wide coverstitch with the needle tension loosened and the stitch lengthened to the maximum. The foot pressure was lowered so that the fabric could be turned in tight curves and diminishing circles.

Medium Blue Fabric

■ Embroider the appliqué design letters **A, B, C** from the embroidery disc: choose whichever fabric you prefer to showcase against your blue fabric. Cut out each letter carefully and stitch to the blue squares after they are cut, positioning the letters at a jaunty angle. Refer to the color reference diagram for the position of the blue squares.

Striped Fabric

■ Cut two $4^{1}/_{4}$-inch (11.5cm) strips selvage to selvage for the top and bottom borders of the quilt. Cut three $4^{1}/_{2}$-inch (11.5cm) strips selvage to selvage for the side borders: join the three strips along the short ends, matching the stripes.

Dark Blue Fabric

■ Cut two $1^{7}/_{8}$-inch (5cm) strips of blue fabric for the top and bottom flange.

■ Cut three $1^{7}/_{8}$-inch (5cm) strips of blue fabric for the side flanges, joining strip ends at a 45-degree angle. Cut the joined strip in half.

■ Cut five $2^{1}/_{4}$-inch (6cm) strips of blue fabric for the binding, joining at a 45-degree angle.

DIRECTIONS

Piecing Your Quilt Center

- Once your fabrics have been embellished, cut the red, gold and green fabrics into 6¹/₂-inch (16.5cm) strips, selvage to selvage. Follow the quilt piecing diagram key for individual fabric cutting. Each dotted line represents a 6-inch (15cm) finished square; add ¹/₄-inch (0.75cm) seam allowances to all the edges that are to be joined.

- Join all the pieces according to the quilt piecing diagram key using a narrow 5-thread stitch. You only need to trim any whiskers of fabric that may be poking out, not trim any fabric. Press intersecting seam allowances away from one another. Since this quilt is for a child, strength and durability are guaranteed with this stitch.

Adding the Flanges

- Fold and press the dark blue fabric in half lengthwise for the flanges with wrong sides together. Stitch one of the shorter flange strips to the top of quilt body, aligning all the raw edges and again using the narrow 5-thread stitch to sew all the layers together. Trim off excess at ends. Press well, leaving the flange lying flat. Repeat for the bottom and then for each side flange, using the joined flange strips along the sides.

Adding the Borders

- Start adding the borders at the upper right-hand side of the quilt. With 12 inches (30cm) of border extending below the lower corner, line up the border strip and the side of the quilt. Leaving the extended border unstitched, stitch to the bottom of the quilt; trim any excess border fabric at the top only. Press the seams to the outside of the quilt. Next stitch the top border strip from the upper left corner edge of

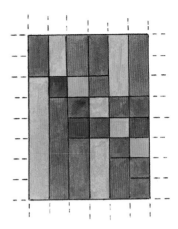

Follow the quilt piecing diagram key for individual fabric cutting. Each dotted line represents a 6-inch finished square; add ¹/₄ inch seam allowances to all the edges that are to be joined.

Take one of the shorter flange strips and stitch to the top of the quilt body; aligning all the raw edges sew all the layers together. Repeat for the bottom and then each side flange.

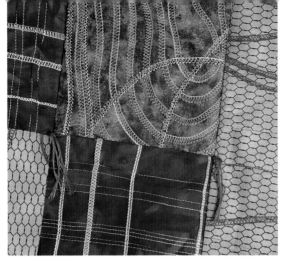

ABC quilt detail—Anne.

the quilt back to the edge of the border fabric. Press and repeat for the remaining two sides working counterclockwise around the quilt. Once the fourth border strip is attached, stitch the remaining 12 inches (30cm) strip of the first border to the body and press.

Quilt Backing

- To make the quilt backing, use your usual method. Ensure that the backing fabric and batting extend at least 4 inches (10cm) past the outer edges. Layer the backing fabric (right side down), the batting and quilt top (right side up). Baste well, or, if you prefer, use safety pins; start at the center and work out to the edges, keeping the layers smooth and unrippled.

- Quilt as you prefer; I stitched in the ditch around the blocks and between the rows first, since it allows the edges of the quilt to be held down with little fuss. I "tied" the quilt with hand embroidery thread though it was technically unnecessary. Work random straight machine stitching sewn in long curves on the striped border to take some of the angular look from the quilt.

Adding the Binding

- Press the binding along the length, wrong sides together. Cut a small square out of each corner of your quilt top and apply a small amount of liquid seam sealant, drying thoroughly. This allows you to serge off

Start adding the borders from the upper right hand side of the quilt. With 12 inches (30cm) extending below corner, line up the border strip and the side of the quilt, leaving the last 12 inches (30cm) unstitched.

and on the edge of your quilt with no added bulk. Open out the binding and position its inner edge along the intended seam at the edge of the quilt with the binding strip extending beyond the quilt edge. With binding uppermost on the front of the quilt, attach with a narrow 5-thread seam and overcast seam, mitering each corner as you go.

- Fold the binding to the back of the quilt and slipstitch in place by hand. Label and date your quilt.

STITCHES AND THREADS

Red Fabric

- 3-thread narrow, 3-thread rolled hem and 3-thread wide stitch using **YLI Jeans Stitch**™ alternating with Sulky variegated 30wt. Rayon™ in the upper looper, Sulky variegated 30wt. Rayon™ in both the needle and lower looper.

- Narrow 5-thread seam and overcast stitch for quilt construction with regular cone thread.

- Triple, wide and narrow coverstitch with Sulky variegated 30wt. Rayon™ in the needles and regular cone thread in the chain looper.

Gold Fabric

- Wide and narrow coverstitch with **YLI Colors**™ thread in the needles and chain looper.

Green Fabric

- Wide coverstitch with **YLI Colors**™ thread in the needles. In the chainstitch looper, **YLI Candlelight**™ was alternated with **Sulky Poly Deco Neon** thread to match the fabric.

Medium Blue Fabric

- Appliqué letters were embroidered with an embroidery machine using variegated gold thread in the needle and white bobbin thread.

- With sewing machine, straight stitch for in-the-ditch quilting with polyester sewing thread.

Anne's Art Quilt—"Out of the Blue"

The art quilt challenge was always one I anticipated with pleasure and saved till last, a bit like eating your favorite meal and keeping the best food on the plate so you can appreciate it most. Nancy and I had a very casual brief, basically "no holds barred" serger techniques incorporating a machine embroidery design (if we wanted) to create our art quilt. I think the hardest thing for me, as always, was not to get too carried away. I am very much a "more is more" girl than a "less is more" girl.

As with any art piece, please understand that, while I will try to make it reproducible for you, it is really about designing your own art quilt from a series of different processes and techniques, using your unique design for your own "Designer Original."

ABOUT "OUT OF THE BLUE"

■ Very retro, "Out of the Blue" was designed with texture, dimension, and curves in mind. I wanted to showcase the flexibility of the serger as a textile art tool, not just equipment for garment construction and traditional embellishment. I also wanted to emphasize the other tools I use in my textile art, in concert with the serger, namely the embroidery machine and computer software that make any design a candidate for change and adventure. I am sure I am one of many people with this sewing armory at their fingertips, rarely integrating all the elements. This is a slightly wedge-shaped quilt, wider at the top and tapering somewhat at the bottom

MATERIALS

5 to 10 yards (5 to 10 meters) 1-inch (2.5cm) wide synthetic horsehair braid; it may be called crinoline, if purchased from millinery suppliers.

Background fabric of your color preference and dimension.

Flannel fabric as batting.

Backing fabric.

Marking equipment for design transfer (pencils, pen, and chalk), whatever is appropriate for your fabric color and design

Husqvarna Viking Embroidery #128, *Flowers and Fashions*, by Lena Mattsson design numbers 5,6, and 10.

Decorative buttonhole designs (Anne used pre-digitized designs from Husqvarna Viking Customizing software).

Stabilizer and embroidery needles to suit the weight of your fabric and density of embroidery design.

A variety of solid and variegated embroidery threads in differing weights of cotton, rayon, and polyester. Match your machine bobbin thread to either the fabric or the embroidery thread color (see below for actual threads used).

Hoop for embroidery.

Embroidery editing software.

Hand embroidery 6-strand floss and needle.

- I selected a very large embroidery design from Husqvarna Viking Embroidery #128, *Flowers and Fashions*, by Lena Mattsson.

- I selected Design #5 for use as dimensional flowers, as well as Design #6 which had numerous circular elements, all nesting within a large design or loosely interweaving with one another. Design # 10 was a sinuous design echoing the curved design elements I chose to complement the overall design concept.

- Design #5: Edit the top two flowers out of the design and re-size to fit the smallest hoop possible. Save to file.

- Design #6: Edit the designs into the individual colors. Save to file as separate colors and individual shapes if you prefer.

- Design #10: Save the design "as is" in 3 separate files; because of the size of the design, it is automatically split into 3 files.

- Buttonholes: Save your preferred buttonhole to file.

- Print out templates of each of your embroidery designs and button-holes for design of your quilt.

- Convert your saved design files into the machine format appropriate for your embroidery machine.

DESIGN PREPARATION

- Work a general design idea out on paper the same size as your art quilt or create at the computer to scale. Build the design up from the fabric first: plan the buttonholes in a logical sequence for the horsehair braid to be threaded through. Work out where your embroidery designs and dimensional flowers will be, ensuring they are not too heavy or too large for your quilt and scatter your designs throughout the quilt. Do not be too structured or the quilt will lose spontaneity.

- Mark serger design lines on the batting (flannel) for those designs which will showcase the chain looper thread.

- Baste the fabric and batting together, working this top part of the quilt as one piece of fabric. Transfer any designs to the quilt with suitable marking equipment.

AT THE EMBROIDERY MACHINE

- Using 3-thread overlock fabric (refer to Chapter 3, Serger Tapas, and "At the Serger," below), embroider Design #5 for as many 3-D flowers as you want. Overlay hand-painted silk chiffon over some of the 3-thread overlock fabric, cutting back in some petals of the flower and around the flower perimeter. Tease out any errant fibers from the serger fabric for a more organic look. Working according to your design plan, embroider the design elements of Design #6 directly onto your suitable stabilized fabric.

- Work Design #10 as three separate sections, offsetting the design both horizontally and vertically, as though it had been torn apart. Join the separated elements with your preferred Coverstitch.

AT THE SERGER

- Using a narrow 3-thread stitch, edge both sides of the horsehair braid.

- Work Triple, Wide and Narrow Coverstitch from both the wrong and right sides of your fabrics for maximum texture and dimension, matching the thread color to one of your embroidery designs for continuity. For very tight circles, lower the presser foot pressure.

- Make a variety of 3-thread overlock fabric (refer to Chapter 3, Serger Tapas) in your preferred colors.

- Create Coverstitch Cable (refer to Chapter 3, Serger Tapas) using serger cords and funky fibers and stitch it loosely meandering to and from the 3-D flowers.

ASSEMBLY AND CONSTRUCTION

- When your embroideries and serger stitches have been completed to your satisfaction, lay your backing fabric, and the top part of your quilt sandwich together right sides. Add a rod pocket for hanging your quilt at this time if that is your choice. Sew quilt and backing edges together, leaving an opening along one side sufficient to turn the quilt through. Turn through to right side. Topstitch the opening closed at the machine, continuing around the entire edge of the quilt.

- Stitch out the buttonhole markings on your quilt top and embroider through all layers with the bobbin thread matching either the embroidery thread or the fabric backing.

- Thread the horsehair braid through the buttonholes in your pre-planned sequence, twisting the horsehair on itself to create more curlicues as you go. Hand- or machine-stitch in place with a few discreet stitches.

- Quilt by hand using all 6 strands of embroidery floss in a pattern or design that is pleasing to you. Do not be too concerned about having all the stitches absolutely even, this is meant to be a free expression and irregular or uneven stitching is the better option.

- Add machine or serger quilting, if you choose.

- Sign, date, and label your art quilt.

Anne's art quilt, "Out of the Blue."

STITCHES AND THREADS

- 3-thread narrow overedge on horsehair braid with 12 wt. Sulky Blendables™ in upper looper, solid color rayon thread in needle and lower looper.

- Triple, Wide and Narrow Coverstitch worked from the wrong and right sides of the fabric with Sulky Variegated™ or 12 wt. Sulky Blendables™ embroidery threads in the chain looper and polyester embroidery threads in the needles.

- Embroidery designs and buttonholes stitched in a harmonious color theme with threads selected at random.

Sources and Suppliers

THREAD SUPPLIERS

YLI threads and ribbons from YLI Corporation. Contact vsmith@ylicorp.com for a dealer near you in North America and UK; cottononcreations@bigpond.com.au for suppliers in Australia.

Sulky Threads, Superior Threads: Contact your local fabric store or serger dealer; in North America Sulkyfox@yahoo.com; in UK sales@gs.uk.com; www.superiorthreads.com in North America and UK; www.ggcreations.com.au, Altheas Needles and Threads Online, TextileBoutique.com in Australia

OESD embroidery and metallic threads. Contact your local serger dealer or Oklahoma Embroidery Supply and Design through www.EmbroideryOnline.com and select the dealer locator tab to find a retailer nearest you

STABILIZERS/SPRAYS

Sulky fabric adhesive spray and stabilizers. Use email or Web addresses above or contact your local fabric chain store

Fusible web and water soluble stabilizers. Contact your local serger dealer or the OESD Web address above for a dealer nearest you

GARMENT CHALLENGE PATTERNS:

Thai Coat and Elle Shirt and Pant from The Sewing Workshop, telephone (800) 466-1599, email www.sewingworkshop.com

Kimono Jacket and Vest #1007 and Sahara Vest #1025 from Purrfection Artistic Wearables, telephone (800) 691-4293 or email at www.purrfection.com

Bolero Jacket #5106 from Loes Hinse Design, telephone (888) 554-LOES or email at www.loeshinsedesign.com

Vogue #7799, Sleeveless Shell, purchase from your local fabric chain store.

Easy Street Jacket by Four Corners

Fine Wools Direct: fwd@finewoolsdirect.com.au summer-weight wools.

Silksational: sales@silksational.com.au hand-dyed silk for pockets, P.A.W. prints the Big Shirt, silk fabrics on Art quilt.

Independent Designer's patterns from Perpetual Patterns: p_patterns@yahoo.com

P.A.W. prints "The Big Shirt"; Diane Ericson's "Dragonfly Jacket": The Sewing Workshop "Thai Coat": Lois Hines's Bolero Jacket.

ART QUILT

Poppy floral embroidery design #792 from Oklahoma Embroidery Supply and Design. Email www.embroideryonline.com to order.

Husqvarna Viking Embroidery #128, Flowers and Fashions, by Lena Mattsson.

Husqvarna Viking Professional Plus (customizing and digitizing) www.husqvarnaviking.com

ABC QUILT

ABC . . . 123 appliqué embroidery designs by Rowena Charlton Designs: www.rowenacharlton.com

Metric Equivalents [to the nearest mm, 0.1cm, or 0.01m]

inches	mm	cm	inches	mm	cm	inches	mm	cm
$^1/_8$	3	0.3	9		22.9	30		76.2
$^1/_4$	6	0.6	10		25.4	31		78.7
$^3/_8$	10	1.0	11		27.9	32		81.3
$^1/_2$	13	1.3	12		30.5	33		83.8
$^5/_8$	16	1.6	13		33.0	34		86.4
$^3/_4$	19	1.9	14		35.6	35		88.9
$^7/_8$	22	2.2	15		38.1	36		91.4
1	25	2.5	16		40.6	37		94.0
$1^1/_4$	32	3.2	17		43.2	38		96.5
$1^1/_2$	38	3.8	18		45.7	39		99.1
$1^3/_4$	44	4.4	19		48.3	40		101.6
2	51	5.1	20		50.8	41		104.1
$2^1/_2$	64	6.4	21		53.3	42		106.7
3	76	7.6	22		55.9	43		109.2
$3^1/_2$	89	8.9	23		58.4	44		111.8
4	102	10.2	24		61.0	45		114.3
$4^1/_2$	114	11.4	25		63.5	46		116.8
5	127	12.7	26		66.0	47		119.4
6	152	15.2	27		68.6	48		121.9
7	178	17.8	28		71.1	49		124.5
8	203	20.3	29		73.7	50		127.0

yards	inches	mm
$^1/_8$	4.5	0.11
$^1/_4$	9	0.23
$^3/_8$	13.5	0.34
$^1/_2$	18	0.46
$^5/_8$	22.5	0.57
$^3/_4$	27	0.69
$^7/_8$	31.5	0.80
1	36	0.91

conversion factors

1 mm	=	0.039 inch
1 m	=	3.28 feet
1 m	=	1.09 yards
1 inch	=	25.4 mm
1 foot	=	30.5 cm
1 yard	=	0.91 m
mm	=	millimeter
cm	=	centimeter
m	=	meter

Index

About the Authors

Fiber artist, author, and tutor, **Anne van der Kley** (left) teaches at the International Husqvarna Viking convention and the Janome Institute, and presents original projects at Bernina University, the American Stitches Expo, and the Original Sewing and Craft Expo. She is the author of *The Art of Creative Overlocking* and *Serging Australia—Overlocker Artistry.*

Anne has sewn since she was a teenager, throughout her nursing career, and for her children. Anne's nursing background gives her scope for quirky names to describe what she calls "exploratory" and "developmental" work. She has dubbed herself "The Thread Sergin." Surface embellishment has become her forum. Her signature "Threadfabric" technique and her creations have won her international accolades and prizes, including honorable mention in 2005 and second place in 2004 at the Sulky Challenge, and third place from Amazing Designs, all in the Professional Wearable Art category. Anne lives in Sydney, Australia.

Freelance instructor, Bernina educator, and author, **Nancy Bednar** (right) has written *The Encyclopedia of Sewing Machine Techniques* and *Silk Ribbon Machine Embroidery* and contributed to *Sewing Update, Serging Update, Sew News,* and the Bernina publication "Through the Needle." She also develops projects for the Bernina Web sites.

Learning how to sew at an early age from an after-school park district class, she has explored all aspects of sewing creativity including garment, home decorating, and bridal. Known as the "Serger Queen" at Bernina, she also loves pushing the creative edge on what those machines can do. Nancy loves to teach both consumers and Bernina dealers across the nation, sharing the philosophy of "creativity made easy" to foster and continue the love of sewing in current and future generations.

Nancy lives in La Grange Park, IL with her two children, two dogs, and more yards of fabric, threads, sewing books, and patterns than she can count.